Kay Griffiths

The Piacentini Family History

Tracing Your Italian Ancestors

D0434466

Published by

MELROSE BOOKS

An Imprint of Melrose Press Limited
St Thomas Place, Ely
Cambridgeshire
CB7 4GG, UK
www.melrosebooks.com

FIRST EDITION

Copyright © Kay Griffiths 2011

The Author asserts her moral right to
be identified as the author of this work

ISBN 978 1 907040 56 6

All rights reserved. No part of this publication may be reproduced, stored in a retrieval system, or transmitted, in any form or by any means electronic, mechanical, photocopying, recording or otherwise, without the prior permission of the publishers.

This book is sold subject to the condition that it shall not, by way of trade or otherwise, be lent, re-sold, hired out or otherwise circulated without the publisher's prior consent in any form of binding or cover other than that in which it is published and without a similar condition including this condition being imposed on the subsequent purchaser.

Printed and bound in Great Britain by:
CPI Antony Rowe. Chippenham, Wiltshire

MIX
Paper
FSC FSC® C013604

DEDICATION

I would like to thank family and friends for their support and enthusiasm.

CONTENTS

INTRODUCTION

I originally started researching my family tree for my mother who wanted to know where her father came from in Italy. My mother Doris Rose Piacentini knew she had Aunts who were on the stage but did not know exactly which shows they were in.

I started by visiting the London Records Births/Deaths/Marriages and came away with three generations of English-born ancestors – grandfather, great-grandfather, great-great-grandfather and their families. Italian names are not usually common names in the records, which makes tracing a lot easier.

My mother, her brother and sisters were all interested in their history. Four of the family were alive and two brothers deceased when I started to write up my research.

My cousins were interested and this led me to publish my findings. These books were completed for family only and four editions produced which are the basis of my book.

My two sons Stephen and Adrian Griffiths spent time in the summer holidays going to various record offices looking for information. Adrian spent time on holiday with me in Chioggia finding out about where the Piacentini family lived, then travelling to Cambridge going through records and collating information.

My thanks to them all for their interest and support.

CHAPTER ONE

PIACENTINI IN ENGLAND

Northern Italy.

BRANDON JAMES GRIFFITHS

BORN 9th APRIL 2006

SON OF STEPHEN GRIFFITHS

BORN IN BASILDON HOSPITAL, ESSEX

Brandon James Griffiths – photo with his boot.

Stephen and Adrian Griffiths. At the top of a tor in Exmoor, Devon.

Youngest son

```
CERTIFICATE OF BIRTH

ADRIAN GRIFFITHS
MALE
22nd JUNE 1974
HARLOW – REGISTRATION DISTRICT
SUB-DISTRICT HARLOW
```

Eldest son

CERTIFICATE OF BIRTH

STEPHEN GRIFFITHS
MALE
27th FEBRUARY 1971
EPPING – REGISTRATION DISTRICT
HARLOW – SUB DISTRICT

ANDERSON FAMILY TREE

Frederick Sydney Anderson
 B 26 March 1908
 D 30 August 1974
Doris Rose Piacentini
 B 8 March 1909
 D 25 February 1985
 M 20 April 1935

Kay Anderson
 B 11 March 1944
 M 22 October 1966

Michael Anderson
 B 17 August 1946
 Line Ends
 No wife or children

NOTE: A separation order was issued to my mother.

GRIFFITHS FAMILY TREE

Kathleen Anderson B 11 March 1944
Roy E Griffiths B 12 April 1942
M 22 October 1966
St Mary's at Latton Church, Harlow
Marriage
Baptism St Bartholomew Church, South Tottenham

Stephen Griffiths
B 27 February 1971
M Julie Scutchings
Son: Brandon James Griffiths
B 9 April 2006

Adrian Griffiths
22 June 1974
M Victoria Sara Hodkisson
15 October 2001
Deceased both parties
13 September 2003

Bride – Kay Anderson.

CERTIFIED COPY OF AN ENTRY OF MARRIAGE REGISTRATION DISTRICT – EPPING

PARISH CHURCH – ST MARY'S AT LATTON, COUNTY OF ESSEX

DATE 22nd OCTOBER 1966

Roy E Griffiths	24	Bachelor	Builder	25 Roland Road	Herbert Arthur Griffiths
Kathleen Anderson	22	Spinster	Secretary	57 Felmongers	Frederick Sydney Anderson

Kay Anderson with Carol Oliver (now Ellis) and Rosemary Bush, my bridesmaids,
who were not married like myself when the photograph was taken.
The best man, my brother Michael Anderson.

Kay Griffiths and Brenda Griffiths with Ian.

JOHN PIACENTINI

John Piacentini is the last member of the family to hold the name Piacentini. John and his wife Doreen were married for 50 years and celebrated this on 3rd June 2000 by having a holiday in Crete for their Golden Wedding. John Piacentini is now deceased. July 2010.

John Piacentini served in the British Royal Navy. He served on Submarines and held the rank of Petty Officer. John Piacentini celebrated his 70th Birthday in July 1999.

Approximately 200 years of the Piacentini family are researched and recorded. The family continues with descendants who no longer hold the name.

Family Achievements

- Joyce Sutterby nee Piacentini – Dip Ed, B.Sc. Teacher Private Sector – Head level. Own business.
- Suzanne Smith nee Piacentini – SRN Staff Nurse Charing Cross Hospital.
- Ann Gold – Teacher. Teaching Certificate Secondary level. BA (Hons.) English and History.
- Kay Griffiths – Lecturer Business Administration/Information Technology. Cert Ed F & HE, Post Graduate Qualification, T Dip WP, LCGI Business Administration – Degree, LCGI Training and Development – Degree. FSBT.
- Terry Ellis – B.Sc (Hons) Eng. Senior Management Posts Canada.
- Michael Anderson – Structural Detailer Management Posts, Own Business.
- Les Pearson – Management level, Bedford County Council.
- Ken Pearson – Technical Director Post.
- Geraldine Pearson – Acting Superintendant of Police, Bedfordshire Police.
- Don Pearson – Banking – Management level. Consultant own business.
- Gary Pearson – Middle Management level Highways Division, Bedford County Council.

Young Adults – children of the above cousins

- Debbie Gold – B.Sc. Eng. Chartered Engineer – Senior Management level.
- Lisa Gold – BA Hons 1st class Economics MA
- Adrian Griffiths – BA (Hons) Economics Upper 2 1. CIMA Chartered Institute of Management Accountants. Senior Management level. Deceased 29 years.
- Stephen Griffiths – Senior Management – Retail. British Judo Champion – Kata's Gold Medal two years, 1988 and 1989. 1995 Silver Medal 2 Kata's.
- Sharon Ellis – Canadian Law Degree.
- Sean Ellis – Theatre Management Edmonton and Calgary Canada. Appeared in show in the Theatre in Vancouver.
- Tommy Pearson – Management level travelling over the world. Deceased 25 years.

The cousins are still in touch today and meet up for family functions.

The descendants of the Piacentini line are now all in different professions and types of employment and no one has carried on the trade of glass-blowing or silvering.

Ann Gold's Wedding.
Bride Ann Gold and Bridesmaid Kay Anderson.
June Wedding prior to my October Wedding.

Carol and Terry Ellis 1966 Wedding.

Doris Rose Piacentini - Age 21 years
Deceased.

Doris Rose Piacentini - Age 19 years.
Deceased.

Irene Piacentini and George Ellis - Both deceased.

John and Violet Piacentini.
Both deceased and their son John Piacentini is deceased.

George Piacentini and Betty.
Married and divorced - both deceased.

Dolly and Albert Piacentini.
Dolly deceased and Uncle Bert is still alive at the time of writing and publishing this book.

Doris Rose Piacentini and Frederick Sydney Anderson.

Ernest Piacentini Family Tree

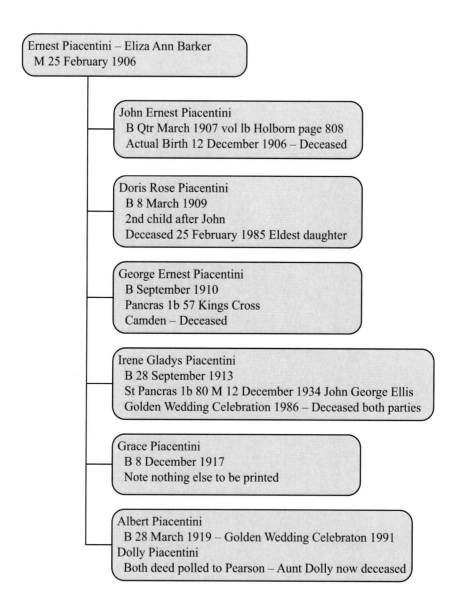

Ernest Piacentini – Eliza Ann Barker
M 25 February 1906

John Ernest Piacentini
B Qtr March 1907 vol lb Holborn page 808
Actual Birth 12 December 1906 – Deceased

Doris Rose Piacentini
B 8 March 1909
2nd child after John
Deceased 25 February 1985 Eldest daughter

George Ernest Piacentini
B September 1910
Pancras 1b 57 Kings Cross
Camden – Deceased

Irene Gladys Piacentini
B 28 September 1913
St Pancras 1b 80 M 12 December 1934 John George Ellis
Golden Wedding Celebration 1986 – Deceased both parties

Grace Piacentini
B 8 December 1917
Note nothing else to be printed

Albert Piacentini
B 28 March 1919 – Golden Wedding Celebraton 1991
Dolly Piacentini
Both deed polled to Pearson – Aunt Dolly now deceased

ERNEST PIACENTINI

Ernest Piacentini did not have the trade of his father as did his brother Joseph. It is documented that Ernest had various types of employment.

By looking at the Marriage Certificate of Irene Gladys Piacentini you will see that Ernest was at the time employed as Hotel Maintenance Man on 12th December 1936. He was employed at the Carlton Hotel in London.

On his death certificate he is shown as Retired Stoker, Ministry of Works.
Ernest Piacentini was married twice. He married Eliza Ann Barker, who had a large family. Her sister Elizabeth Ann Barker married Maurice Nunas (often spelt Morris Nunas) and they emigrated to Manitoba, Canada with their children and the family are still in Canada spread across the States. Their descendants are still in touch with the author. They ran a farm in Carmen, Manitoba and a separate tree is available. The Nunas family tree is published in Canada.

Eliza Piacentini was cremated and her ashes are at Golders Green Crematorium, London.

Ernest Piacentini married for the second time after his wife died; he married Ethel. Ethel Piacentini was related to his son's wife, Dolly Piacentini. He remained married to Ethel until his death.

Ernest Piacentini did not serve as a soldier in any World Wars but all three of his sons served in the British Army during the 2nd World War. Bert was the only one who actually saw active service abroad. Bert fought throughout the war in the 8th Army in North Africa and up through Italy and finally into Austria at the war end. His four campaign medals are now held by his son, Leslie Pearson.

Ernest Piacentini brought up his children and is remembered by all the brothers and sisters for all the fun they had with their friends, cousins, aunts and uncles. 'Pop', as he was known by all the family, is remembered for all the fun parties and happenings that went on throughout their lives. This great sense of family has continued on down through his children to their sons and daughters. All the cousins were brought up in this great atmosphere.

Albert Piacentini – 1944 Monte Casino.

Leslie Piacentini.

Ernest Piacentini with Leslie Piacentini in the white.

Mr & Mrs A.L.F. Pearson
Request the pleasure of your company

KAY, ROY, STEPHEN AND ADRIAN

At their **Golden Wedding**

RSVP

NOTE: This is a copy of the original invitation with the address omitted as it was held in a very nice venue, the home of one of the sons and his wife.

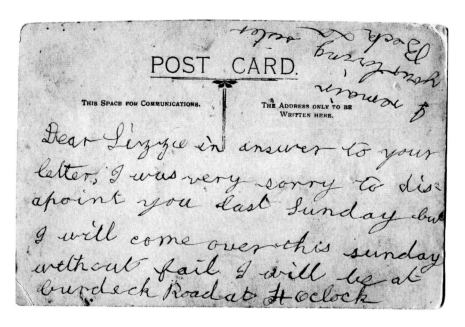

Reverse side of postcard of which the photograph below is the front.
Eliza's sister has written to her.

Rebecca – left.
Eliza – right – Gt Grandmother – Barker.
Wife of Ernest Piacentini.

Great Western Railways Society Document.

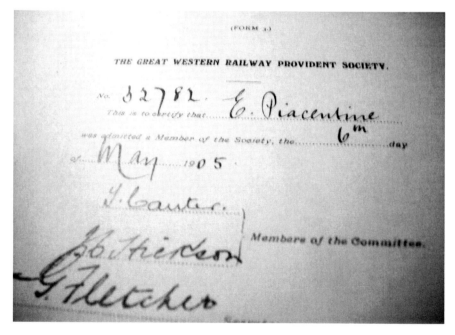

Great Western Railways document signed E Piacentini. Grandmother Eliza.

COPY OF DEATH CERTIFICATE FOR JOHN PIACENTINI

John Piacentini – brother to Doris and Rene.

Entry 1st April 1979
Stoke Mandeville Hospital Aylesbury
John Ernest Piacentini
Capstan Lathe Operator (retired)
Myocardi Infaction
Certified by C Farrant MB
Signature of informant J Piacentini

BIRTH OF ERNEST PIACENTINI MY GRANDFATHER

Copy of original certificate.

6 December 1885	Ernest	Boy	John Piacentini	Elizabeth Piacentini Formerly Mencarini	Glass-blower	J Piacentini Father 60 Victoria Dwellings Clerkenwell	13 January 1886	William David Price Registrar

MARRIAGE CERTIFICATE

Copy of the original information on the marriage certificate.

Date	Name	Age	Status	Occupation	Father
20 April 1935	Frederick Sydney Anderson	27	Bachelor	Store Keeper	Sydney John Anderson
	Doris Rose Piacentini	26	Spinster	Mantle Worker	Ernest Piacentini

This information is extracted from my mother's marriage certificate.

The marriage took place at St Bartholomew's Church, Stamford Hill, Tottenham.

DEATH CERTIFICATE

The style of death certificate changes between the death of my grandfather, which is more the style of a marriage certificate and my mother's, which is portrait instead of landscape A5 size.

Ernest Piacentini

Death 9th October 1951

It does state the address which is where my grandfather lived and brought up his family.

He was 65 years old

Retired stoker Ministry of Works

Cause of Death Angina Pectoris

Cardio Vascular Renal Disease

Hypertensive Disease

Certified by his Doctor M J Cronin M.B.

D R Anderson

Daughter In attendance plus the address given

(D R Anderson is my mother)

NOTE: This certificate is not 100 years old; therefore I have not printed the original even though my grandfather, mother and father are dead.

DEATH CERTIFICATE

Doris Rose Anderson
Maiden surname: Piacentini
Sex: Female
Date and place of Birth: 8th March 1909, Edmonton, Enfield
Date and place of Death: 25th February 1985. Herts. and Essex Hospital, Bishops Stortford
Widow of Frederick Sydney Anderson
Name and Surname of informant: Kathleen Griffiths
Qualification: Daughter
Usual address: 20 Twyford Gardens, Bishops Stortford. Herts.
Cause of death: Carcinomatosis Gastric Carcinoma
Certified by: P. Acherson M.B.
Signed by: K Griffiths, 25th February 1985
The signature of the registrar M. Smith

NOTE: 1985 - my mother's death and although she would have been almost 100 years old I have not printed the certificate.

DEATH CERTIFICATE

30th August 1974
57 Felmongers, Harlow
Frederick Sydney Anderson
Male
Instrument maker retired
Name of informant: Doris Rose Anderson
Widow of deceased present at death
Usual address records the same address as above
Cause of death: Cerebrovascular Accident, Arteriosclerosis,
Mycardial Infarct

Certified by my father's doctor MRCS
Signed by D R Anderson and by the registrar.

Coppelia.

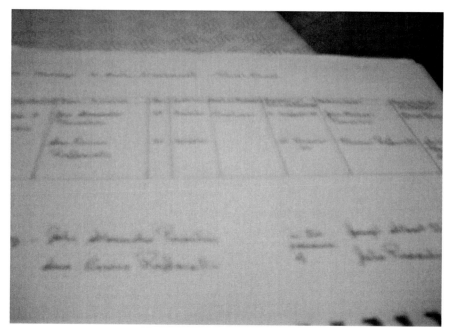

Photo of author's handwritten certificate of marriage of John Alexander Piacentini.

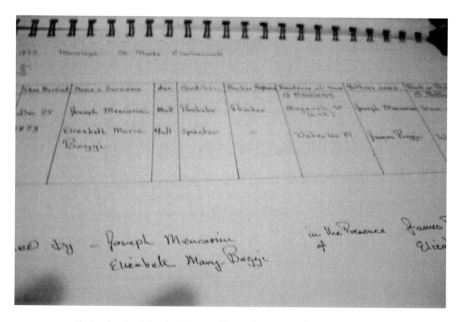

Photo of author's handwritten certificate of marriage of Joseph Mencarini.

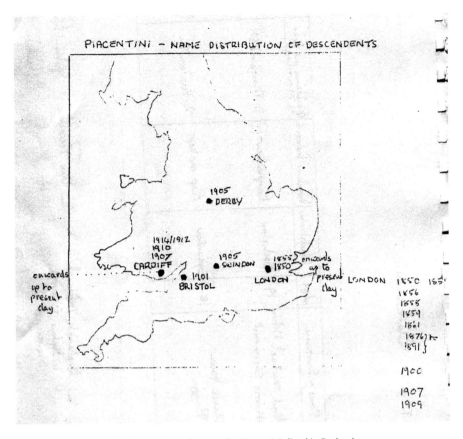

Distribution Map of where the Piacentinis lived in England.

COPY OF THE INFORMATION ON THE ORIGINAL MARRIAGE CERTIFICATE

Date	Name	Age	Status	Occupation	Father
12 December 1936	John George Ellis	26	Bachelor	Engineer	Charles Ernest Ellis
	Irene Gladys Piacentini	23	Spinster	Machinist	Ernest Piacentini

THIS IS THE LAST WILL OF ME DORIS ROSE
PIACENTINI of 57 FELMONGERS HARLOW in the county of
Essex whereby I REVOKE all wills and testamentary dispositions
previously made by me.

1. I APPOINT MICHAEL ANDERSON of 57 Felmongers Harlow afore-
    said to be the SOLE EXECUTOR of this my Will.

2. I DESIRE that my body be cremated.

3. I GIVE all my property both real and personal whatsoever and whereso-
    ever situate Equally between my son the said MICHAEL ANDERSON
    and my daughter KATHLEEN GRIFFITHS of 20 Twyford Gardens,
    Bishop's Stortford in the County of Hertford.

4. I DECLARE that any Executor or Trustee of this my Will (whether
    hereby or hereafter appointed) being engaged in any profession or busi-
    ness may charge and be paid for all work or acts done by him or his firm
    in connection with the proof of this my Will and any codicil hereto and
    the carrying out of the provisions and trusts hereof including work or acts
    which an Executor or Trustee not being engaged in such profession or
    business could have done personally.

IN WITNESS whereof I have hereunto set my hand this seventh day of
February One Thousand nine hundred and seventy five.

SIGNED by the said

DORIS ROSE ANDERSON

As her last Will in our presence and

By us in the presence of her and of each other:

**NOTE: This is an unsigned copy of the signed will by Doris Rose
Anderson nee Piacentini by her solicitors.**

JOSEPH (GUISEPPE) PIACENTINI

MARRIAGE OF JOSEPH PIACENTINI

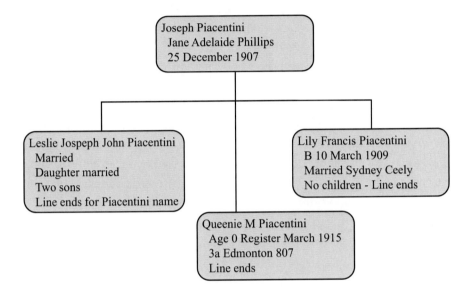

Joseph Piacentini – son of John Michael Piacentini – father of Leslie Joseph John and Lily Francis Piacentini.

Joseph was the only son with his father's trade of glass-blower. He worked for Cossors and served an apprenticeship with them. He became a Manager of the Cossors Highgate Works. His wife Janie (Aunt Janie) died during the Second World War and was cremated at Golders Green Crematorium.

Joseph and his brother Ernest Piacentini were extremely close to each other and very good friends. Their wives were friends as well as sisters-in-law. All the children – cousins – were brought up in a very close family circle. They were always together throughout their lives for family parties, Sunday teas, celebrations, and family days out.

It is through these two brothers that the family of cousins remained with the same attitude to life and all brought their own children up in a close circle which even remains today. Over the years there have been so many family celebrations/occasions and cousins of their sons and daughters are today still good friends as well as relations.

The photograph below is of Lily Francis Piacentini with her mother Jane Piacentini – Aunt Janie to the rest of the family. Lily is about 18 months in this photograph. The photograph of her alone was taken when she was slightly older and she thought she was about five years of age when this was taken. Lily gave these photographs in order that they might be included in the family tree along with the marriage certificate of her parents. As she had no children the line ends from the female side of her family but continues on with her brother Leslie who married and had a daughter who married and had two sons. The name of Piacentini was changed by Deed Poll by Leslie Piacentini and his wife to Pearson. Their daughter married and had two sons and the name of Piacentini no longer exists in this family.

Lily Piacentini with her mother Jane Adelaide Phillips.

Lily Piacentini.

This is Lily's handwriting from a gift tag from flowers she sent me – the author
Kay Griffiths on her 21st Birthday.

Wedding gift card from Aunt Lily.

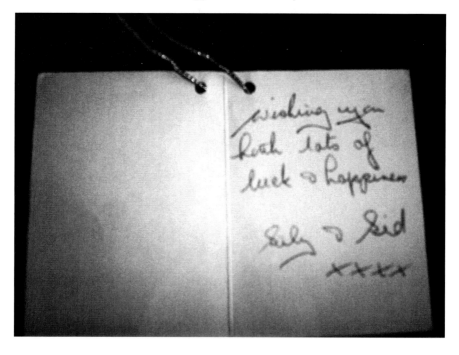

GUISEPPE MENCARINI

BIRTH CIRCA 1818 TUSCANY, ITALY.

BIRTH CERTIFICATE RECORDS HIS DAUGHTER'S BIRTH.

1853 St Andrew's Eastern Holborn
County of Middlesex

Records the birth of Elizabeth
Girl
Joseph Mencarini is recorded as the father
Eliza Mencarini is recorded as the mother formerly Booth
Figure Maker is the father's trade
Parents' address is 49 Baldwin Gardens
24th September 1853 Birth date

NOTE: A lot of information is given on the parents in relation to the address and who the mother's family were, i.e. formerly Booth.

13 September 1853 49 Baldwin Gardens	Elizabeth	Girl	Eliza Mencarini Formerly Booth	Figure Maker	Joseph Mencarini Father 49 Baldwin Gardens	24 September 1853	Signed by Registrar

Frederick Sydney Anderson.
Blitz Fireman WW2.

Frederick Sydney Anderson.
Fire Blitz Fireman WW2 (2nd in row in front of fire engine).

NOTE: The author's family photographs are from inherited documents.

Welsh Line Piacentini

Welsh Piacentini Family Tree

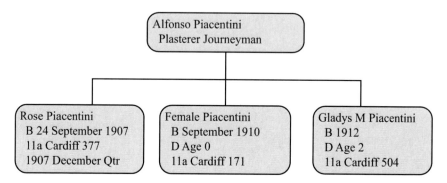

Alfonso Piacentini
Plasterer Journeyman

Rose Piacentini
B 24 September 1907
11a Cardiff 377
1907 December Qtr

Female Piacentini
B September 1910
D Age 0
11a Cardiff 171

Gladys M Piacentini
B 1912
D Age 2
11a Cardiff 504

THE CERTIFICATE FOR THE BIRTH OF ROSE PIACENTINI IS INCLUDED.

I have been unable to fit them into our family tree as it is unproven as yet that they belong there.

In the late 1980s I contacted the Piacentini family in Cardiff and the father-in-law did not want to discuss this although his daughter-in-law thought it would be very interesting.

C J Piacentini 166 Burnham Avenue Llanrumney Cardiff 0222 794664
W Piacentini 1 Ball Close Llanrumney Cardiff 0222 799210
W Piacentini is William Albert and is the father of C J who is Clive John Piacentini.

I have been unable to connect these two to our family by the records available in London!

I filed for the certificate because I thought they might connect to George Piacentini.

I have not checked since that time whether they are still there.

WELSH LINE PIACENTINI – BIRTHS

Piacentini – Gorman

1921	March Quarter	William A	Cardiff 11a 84
1926	Dec Quarter	Alfonso	Cardiff 11a 656
1928	March Quarter	Leonard	Cardiff 11a 645
1929	Dec Quarter	Patricia	Cardiff 11a 567
1930	Dec Quarter	Mary	Cardiff 11a 591

Piacentini – Stoneman

1923	March Quarter	Rose A	Cardiff 11a 689
1925	Dec Quarter	Frederick	Cardiff 11a 601b
1928	Sept Quarter	Louisa	Cardiff 11a 571

Piacentini – McClean

1923	Dec Quarter	Eileen M	Cardiff 11a 719
1925	June Quarter	Maria M	Cardiff 11a 763
1926	Sept Quarter	Winifred R	Cardiff 11a 668
1928	Dec Quarter	Maureen V	Cardiff 11 634
1930	Sept Quarter	Joseph	Cardiff 11a 684

Piacentini – Walters

1931	June Quarter	Wilfred R	Cardiff 11a 621

SWINDON PIACENTINI

Piacentini – Battoni

1926	Dec Quarter	Angelo M	Swindon 5a 42

MARYLEBONE, LONDON – BIRTH UNLINKED TO OUR FAMILY.

Piacentini – Tantardini			
1925	Sept Quarter	Angela	Marylebone 1a 658
1928	Sept Quarter	Mario E	Marylebone 1a 615

The 1900s Marriage Records record the following girls' marriages. So far they are unlinked to the family.

Aunt Lily has told me her middle name is Francis which is Flavia in Italian!

Maria Piacentini		
1907	Dec Quarter	1a Hampstead 1408
1905	March Quarter	7b Derby 721
1905	June Quarter	5a Swindon 57

Flavia Piacentini		
1900	Dec Quarter	1b Holborn 1363

(The reference for this marriage is for the same district as all our family references; the volume 1b is the same, the only difference being in the page no.)

In the Birth Records I found the following Piacentini:-

Roland Piacentini		
1901	Dec Quarter	6a Bristol 1

Frederick Piacentini		
1904	March Quarter	6a Bristol 105

All these Marriages and Births are in the same period of time as those of Ernest and Joseph Piacentini's children's births.

The only other Piacentini I found who did not fit into the family tree as yet was WILLIAM ALPHONSO 1891 Axbridge Sept Qtr 5c 517. This is a birth at the same period of time as Selina Sarah P, Ernest and Joseph's sister and the two Mencarini children.

If he is the Cardiff Alfonso he would have been only 16 years of age! Unlikely!

COPY OF BIRTH CERTIFICATE
CARDIFF – Registration District

24 September 1907	Rose	Girl	Alfonso Piacentini	Rose Piacentini Formerly Balaam	Plasterer Journeyman	R Piacentini Mother 36 Davis Street Cardiff	8 November 1907	CJCotes Registrar

NOTE: I hope I have not offended anyone and would like to say that I had a really nice conversation with the Cardiff Piacentinis a long while ago. We were unable to prove we belonged to each other. I hope you enjoy my book.

Piacentini – Tantardini. I had a really marvellous chat and we had so much in common with relatives in Australia. We discussed our families but did not know if we were related. Many thanks and I hope you like my book.

I would love to hear from you if you think you are the same family.

Ernest Piacentini Family Tree

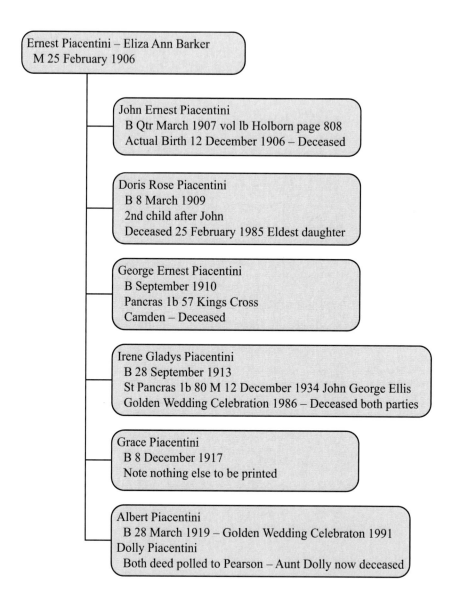

Ernest Piacentini – Eliza Ann Barker
M 25 February 1906

John Ernest Piacentini
  B Qtr March 1907 vol lb Holborn page 808
  Actual Birth 12 December 1906 – Deceased

Doris Rose Piacentini
  B 8 March 1909
  2nd child after John
  Deceased 25 February 1985 Eldest daughter

George Ernest Piacentini
  B September 1910
  Pancras 1b 57 Kings Cross
  Camden – Deceased

Irene Gladys Piacentini
  B 28 September 1913
  St Pancras 1b 80 M 12 December 1934 John George Ellis
  Golden Wedding Celebration 1986 – Deceased both parties

Grace Piacentini
  B 8 December 1917
  Note nothing else to be printed

Albert Piacentini
  B 28 March 1919 – Golden Wedding Celebraton 1991
Dolly Piacentini
  Both deed polled to Pearson – Aunt Dolly now deceased

My grandparents – Ernest and Eliza Piacentini.

JOHN MICHAEL PIACENTINI FAMILY TREE
JOHN MICHAEL PIACENTINI – FATHER OF ERNEST PIACENTINI
AND JOSEPH PIACENTINI

The following are all the known facts about John Michael Piacentini and his family, as per the records.

Church of Birth	St. Andrew's, Holborn, London, Ms 6667 29 vol Baptisms.
	Church records state Birth 12th May 1856, Baptism 8th June 1856, parents John and Martha Piacentini. He was named Michael John Piacentini. The Baptism is recorded in the Mormon Indexes 3rd Edition 1981.
	This is the Church of his parents as per their Marriage Certificate.
Church of Marriage	St. Mark's, Clerkenwell.
	Michael John Piacentini married calling himself John Piacentini and stating his age as 21 years old on 16th October 1875.
	His birth year is 1856 plus 21 years = 1877. He was in fact 19 years of age on his marriage to Elizabeth Mencarini. He was a glass-blower by trade and he would have still been serving an apprenticeship at this age.
	The only other Italian recorded is found in the Baptism records – Susannah Louisa Vacani, born 6th March 1858. Father Andrew Vacani, Hatton Garden, Carver.
	Andrew Vacani signed as a witness to John and Martha Piacentini's wedding and Sadar Vacani was a witness too. 10th September 1855.
Address of John and Elizabeth	2 Easton Street. There is no trace of 2 Easton Street now. The street existed in 1875 as Easton Street, Spafields (W.C.). In 1884 the name changes to Exmouth Street[1], Clerkenwell (W.C.). This property is now known as 36 Exmouth Street.
	In 1872 the property is owned by Harding James-Taylor but no other records have been found. Spafields Charity School was also on this street.

---

1   Farrington Road to Myddleton Street, 1884 Map, M7.

RECORDS CONSULTED:

St. Katherine's House, London – Births and Marriages.

St. Alexander House, London – Deaths.

Parish Records (Baptism and Marriage) St. Mark's, Clerkenwell and St. Andrew's, Holborn – Marriages 1st January 1851-1855 inclusive.

London Street Directories.

London Trade Directories.

London Commerce Directories.

London Court Records.

London Census Records – 1851, 1861, 1871 and 1881.

Only three copies were produced and given to Grace Piacentini – nee Burford, Rene Piacentini – nee Ellis, and John Piacentini. Only Grace Piacentini is alive today and her husband is deceased.

Street Records, Trade Records, Commerce Records and Court Records have all been checked. John and Elizabeth Piacentini did not own a property or a business and he was not listed as a tradesman. Neither John nor Elizabeth went to court for anything.

Research on Church of Marriage – St Mark's, Middleton Sq, Finsbury. Marriages 1879 – 1888, 1897 – 1902, 1902 – 1908.

The only marriages recorded link the three families:

Piacentini
Mencarini
Boggi

The certificates written by hand are copies taken by myself from the Parish Register of Marriages and verify parentage and brothers and sisters with the family. Joseph Piacentini's marriage certificate was supplied by Lily Piacentini (Seely).

The certificates also link addresses:

2 Easton Street	when researched was owned by James Harding who was a tailor – London Street Directories and Trade Directories.
	Maria Jane Boggi – Cap Maker.
2 Easton Street	John and Elizabeth Mencarini (nee Piacentini).
2 Easton Street	on their marriage certificate as the address of both parties.

Certificates link the address of 11 Margaret Street and are signed by other members of families.

Research on Church Records – St Mark's, Middleton Square, Finsbury. Baptismal Records 1849–1871 St Mark's Middleton Square, Finsbury. No Mencarini or Piacentini entries, only Boggi.

June 26th	No 699 Elizabeth Mary. Parents James and Ann Boggi. Occupation Artist in Waxwork.
Born May 1853	Abode Margaret Street.
Nov 11th	No 1063 William James. Parents James and Ann Boggi. Occupation Wax figure maker.
Born Sept 1st 1855	Abode 11 Margaret Street.

Copied from the Church Records, which are handwritten entries.

FRENCH FOREIGN LEGION

19860035/1319/52764
Nom: Piacentini
Prenous: Mathieu
Sex: Male
Date de naissance: 1875/5/19
Eiu de naissance – Haute-Corse; Ortipone
Lieu conservation dossier – Archives nationals;
Site de Fontainebleau
Date devnier document du dossier 1920
Louis XVII

Order de la Legion d'honneur.

Louis Phillippe "King of the French" created the French Foreign Legion on March 10 1831.

Composed of volunteers aged between 18-40 with or without means of identification.

Legion was immediately involved in the conquest of Algeria and passed under Spanish control in 1835.

A second legion was then created and fought in Algeria, in Crimea 1855, Italy 1859, Mexico 1863, France 1870, 1914 – Colonel Rollet headed the regiment, 1939.

Campaigns: Tonkin, Sudan, Dahomeu, Madagascar, Morocco.

1939–1945 – decimated.

13th Half Brigade (Battlelion)
Narvik
Bjervik
Norway

Campaigns: Tunisia, Italy, Provence, Alsace, Germany

1945 – Indo China
Phu tong hua
Colonial Road 4
Dien Bien Phu
Fought to the last man

1954 – Algeria

1962 – present day
2nd Foreign parachute regiment
1st Foreign regiment
Chad operations

1962 – South of France
Corsica
Djibouti
Madagascar
Tahiti
French Guiana

1969 – 1970
2nd Foreign parachute regiment
1st Foreign regiment
Chad operations

May 1978
Kwezi
Zaire

Since 1831:
902 officers
3176 NCOs
And over 30,000 legionnaires have died for France.

CONCLUSION:

Mathieu Piacentini was 18 years of age at the youngest on joining the French Foreign Legion and not over 40 years of age when leaving. Therefore, 1831 March 10th Age 18 means birth 1813 approximately plus age 40 equals 1853 when leaving if he had survived.

We have Michael Piacentini.

Not forgetting Michael Piacentini was a farmer in Italy and had a previous wife and child.

Michael Piacentini had a wife and child in Paris, France, recorded in the records in 1832.

The dates are very close and certainly look as if they are the same family.

QUESTION RAISED:

Was Michael Piacentini who is recorded as married in France, a brother or cousin?

GLASS TRADE IN ENGLAND

Venetian Glass is recorded as being imported in England in 1398.
In 1549, eight glass-blowers arrived in London and established a workshop at Crutched Friars near the Tower of London. Verzelini worked there from 1575 onwards.

Engraved glass with a diamond began in 1560. Twenty years later, it arrived in London. Jacopo Verzelini was named in a patent in 1575. It was for drinking glasses in the style of those made in Murano.

Severe penalties were enforced for absconding workmen. Statutes of the State Inquisition in the mid-1600s had the following:-

- A workman absconding was sent an order to return.
- When he did not obey his relatives were committed to prison.
- If he remained abroad an assassin was sent to kill him.

Two cases are recorded in the Venetian archives.

This still existed in the middle of the eighteenth century.

Glassmakers escaped to Altare near Savona near Genoa. Some went to France, Spain, Germany, Netherlands and UK.

Originally glassmakers came to Venice in 1204 when Crusaders brought them from Byzantium and again in 1453 after Byzantium was captured by the Turks.

Venetian glassmakers were in touch with Alexandria in the 12th century.
The Venetian Marco Polo influenced the design on glass because he had seen Chinese glass designs on his travels.

There is a glass tankard made in Germany in one of my books on glass and it shows coats of arms decorating the tankard. There is a coat of arms with a yellow background and a black eagle with wings upspread and the name Vacari and the figure four in front of it. This name is on my ancestor's marriage certificate. You can find information like this in many types of books; therefore, it is well worth reading the trade books for your ancestor's trade.

I checked the list of exhibitors in the 1851 Great Exhibition in London but did not find my ancestor and that may mean he was not in England then but arrived later. Whether he came from Italy, Chioggia, or from France where his father married again and had another child has not been established yet. Do not overlook checking Exhibitions for your family tradesmen; you might be lucky.

CHIOGGIA – AUGUST 1379

The Genoese in alliance with the Paduans took Chioggia. In December 1379, the Doge and Vetter Pisani who was a freeman blockaded Chioggia. A Peace Treaty was signed in 1381 and the Venetians gained control.

Nobles – Republic of Venice

All nobles were equal under their law. Nobles divided themselves into four ranks:

1 Ennoblement before the year 800 – Old families.
2 Ennoblement after the year 800 – New families.
3 Very new families – ennobled for financial and personal services provided during the 1380 War with Chioggia.
4 Families inscribed in the Golden Book – used in the seventh century

War of Canada and the War of Morea eighteenth century first half.
Entrance was 100,000 ducats – nobles by payment.
Total number of nobles in all categories 6,000 men, women and children.
Cavelerie – hereditary title in a few families.

Age 25 – nobles wore black cloak and a round cap outdoors, whereas Knights wore a gold-threaded stole.

JOHN MICHAEL PIACENTINI – DEATH 1896

Below I give some of the facts about John Michael Piacentini's family:-

Children's ages on his death		
John Alexander	Birth 1877 Dec Qtr	19 years
Eliza Maude	Birth 1880 March Qtr	16 years
Charlotte Martha	Birth 1881 September Qtr	15 years
Joseph Albert Victor	Birth 1883 March Qtr	13 years
George Frederick	Birth 1884 September Qtr Died Age 0 Mar 1885 Holborn 76 1	12 years
Ernest	Birth 1886 March Qtr	10 years
Julia	Birth 1888 September Qtr	8 years
Rosalla Elizabeth	Birth 1890 March Qtr	6 years
Selina Sarah P	Birth 1891 December Qtr	5 years

ELIZABETH MENCARINI/PIACENTINI

Lost her husband when he was aged 40 years and was left with nine children to bring up. John, Eliza, and Charlotte were of an age to gain work. She herself was 42 years of age at the time; she had a baby every eighteen months, and lived to the age of 61 years.

No trace of her ever marrying again. Death is registered as Elizabeth Piacentini age 61 years.

Facts found about the family of John and Elizabeth PIACENTINI are given below:-

JOHN ALEXANDER PIACENTINI (UNCLE JOE)

Married age 29 years. Dead age 32. Marriage was to Ann Louise Raffacellini and was only for three years approximately. His occupation was a Coachman and is verified by the copy of the Marriage Certificate in the following pages. No known children of this marriage.

ADA ELIZABETH

First born child of John Michael and Elizabeth. Dead Age 0. 1876 Death Shoreditch 1c 76.

ELIZA MAUDE (AUNT LIZA)

Married 19 years, three years after her father died. Unable to cross reference the marriage in the records; therefore would need to apply for the certificate to find out who she married.

CHARLOTTE MARTHA (AUNT LOTTIE)

Married aged 30 years. Husband Albert F.P. Kidd. 15 years after her father died. Marriage December 1911. One child only found in the records of this marriage: 1912 Dorothy Kidd although the family call her Doreen. Lottie was a Ballerina. See section on Lottie.

JOSEPH ALBERT VICTOR (UNCLE JOE)

Only one with his father's trade. Apprenticeship with Cossors. Marriage December 25 1907, age 25 to Jane Phillips. Two surviving children Lesley and Lily, one child between, death age 0. Line continues with Lesley and Lily at this stage.

ERNEST (POP2)

Married Eliza Barker. See tree 1906 Mar Qtr. He was aged 20. Line continues with his own children. Eliza Barker had her young brother with her when she married Pop; his name was Charlie and he was brought up by them. He enlisted in the 1914-18 War and was killed in action.

GEORGE FREDERICK

Nothing known in the family about this brother. For an extremely close family who were always together this was unusual!

Death Age 0 Holborn 1b 490 Mar 1855.

JULIA

No trace of a Marriage in England. Died aged 21 years. Ballerina – see section on Julia Piacentini.

ROSALLA ELIZABETH (AUNT DOLLY)

No trace of a Marriage. Other facts about her being on the stage as a speciality act with her sister Lena I have been unable to verify at this stage.

SELINA SARAH P (AUNT LENA)

No trace of a Marriage. See comments above.

---

2   Pop is short for Papa. Pop used instead of Papa – more French than Italian and not English.

GIOVANNI PIACENTINI

Death 1904 Mar Qtr Shoreditch – Age 77

Grandchildren	Age on Grandfather's death
John Alexander	27 years
Eliza Maude	24 years
Charlotte Martha	23 years
Joseph Albert Victor	21 years
George Frederick	Died age 0
Ernest	18 years
Julia	16 years
Rosalla Elizabeth	14 years
Selina Sarah	13 years

All are of an age to gain work at 14 and above. Selina possibly started work!
John Alexander died five years later.
Eliza Maude married at 19.
Lottie in *Coppelia* two years later.
Joseph married three years later.
George unknown.
Ernest married two years later.
Julia in *Coppelia* two years later.
Rosalla Elizabeth – nothing known.
Selina Sarah – nothing known.

Remaining ladies:-
Martha Piacentini.
Two daughters Teresa age 47 and Elizabeth 46.
No trace of Maria Louisa. Marriages not yet known.
Elizabeth Piacentini daughter-in-law.

MARRIAGE OF JOHN PIACENTINI AND ELIZABETH MENCARINI

COPY OF ORIGINAL CERTIFICATE

October 16 1875	John Piacentini	21	Bachelor	Glass-blower	2 Easton Street	John Piacentini	Looking Glass Maker
	Elizabeth Mencarini	22	Spinster			Joseph Mencarini	Wax worker

JOHN PIACENTINI
AND ELIZABETH MENCARINI

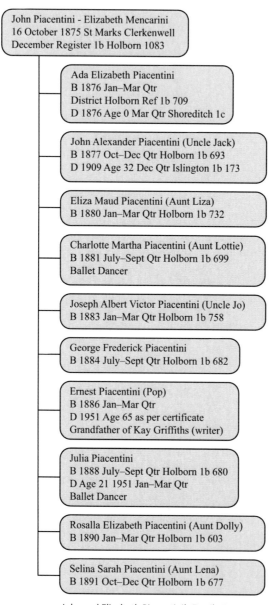

John Piacentini - Elizabeth Mencarini
16 October 1875 St Marks Clerkenwell
December Register 1b Holborn 1083

Ada Elizabeth Piacentini
B 1876 Jan–Mar Qtr
District Holborn Ref 1b 709
D 1876 Age 0 Mar Qtr Shoreditch 1c

John Alexander Piacentini (Uncle Jack)
B 1877 Oct–Dec Qtr Holborn 1b 693
D 1909 Age 32 Dec Qtr Islington 1b 173

Eliza Maud Piacentini (Aunt Liza)
B 1880 Jan–Mar Qtr Holborn 1b 732

Charlotte Martha Piacentini (Aunt Lottie)
B 1881 July–Sept Qtr Holborn 1b 699
Ballet Dancer

Joseph Albert Victor Piacentini (Uncle Jo)
B 1883 Jan–Mar Qtr Holborn 1b 758

George Frederick Piacentini
B 1884 July–Sept Qtr Holborn 1b 682

Ernest Piacentini (Pop)
B 1886 Jan–Mar Qtr
D 1951 Age 65 as per certificate
Grandfather of Kay Griffiths (writer)

Julia Piacentini
B 1888 July–Sept Qtr Holborn 1b 680
D Age 21 1951 Jan–Mar Qtr
Ballet Dancer

Rosalla Elizabeth Piacentini (Aunt Dolly)
B 1890 Jan–Mar Qtr Holborn 1b 603

Selina Sarah Piacentini (Aunt Lena)
B 1891 Oct–Dec Qtr Holborn 1b 677

John and Elizabeth Piacentini's Family Tree.

THREE SONS OF
JOHN AND ELIZABETH PIACENTINI

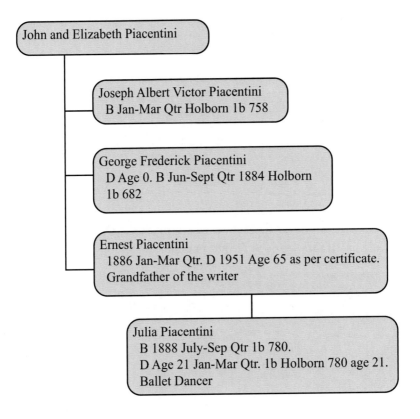

John and Elizabeth Piacentini

Joseph Albert Victor Piacentini
B Jan-Mar Qtr Holborn 1b 758

George Frederick Piacentini
D Age 0. B Jun-Sept Qtr 1884 Holborn
1b 682

Ernest Piacentini
1886 Jan-Mar Qtr. D 1951 Age 65 as per certificate.
Grandfather of the writer

Julia Piacentini
B 1888 July-Sep Qtr 1b 780.
D Age 21 Jan-Mar Qtr. 1b Holborn 780 age 21.
Ballet Dancer

NOTE: Three sons of John and Elizabeth Piacentini.
Julia, daughter of Ernest Piacentini. Ballet dancer, deceased at 21 years old.

JOHN & ELIZABETH PIACENTINI'S
TWO YOUNGEST DAUGHTERS

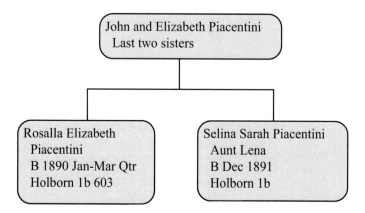

John and Elizabeth Piacentini
Last two sisters

Rosalla Elizabeth
Piacentini
B 1890 Jan-Mar Qtr
Holborn 1b 603

Selina Sarah Piacentini
Aunt Lena
B Dec 1891
Holborn 1b

NOTE: These two sisters have not shown up in any documentation, therefore I cannot establish if they were ballerinas or dancers.

PIACENTINI LINK TO MENCARINI

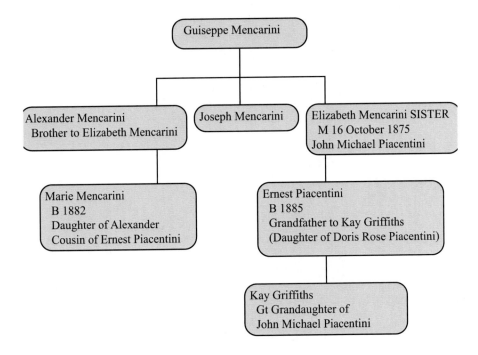

Guiseppe Mencarini

Alexander Mencarini
Brother to Elizabeth Mencarini

Joseph Mencarini

Elizabeth Mencarini SISTER
M 16 October 1875
John Michael Piacentini

Marie Mencarini
B 1882
Daughter of Alexander
Cousin of Ernest Piacentini

Ernest Piacentini
B 1885
Grandfather to Kay Griffiths
(Daughter of Doris Rose Piacentini)

Kay Griffiths
Gt Grandaughter of
John Michael Piacentini

Marie Mencarini lived with John Michael Piacentini.

MEDAL CARDS – MENCARINI

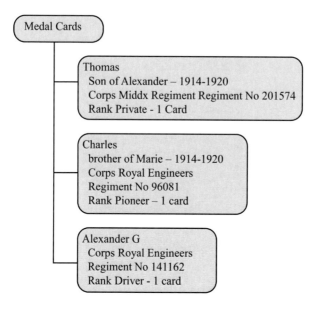

Six year gap between Carolina Maria Anna and Joseph.

NOTE: Joseph Cardinale (father: Joseph Cardinale) Farmer b. 1804 c. 1804.

MICHAEL ANGELO MENCARINI

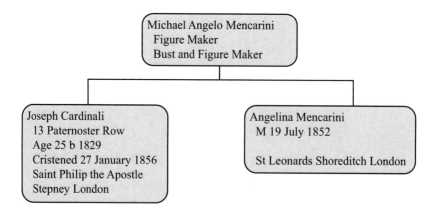

NOTE: Type of error in documents on spelling for Joseph Cardinali.

Sixth Child of Napolene Emperor I
2nd Marriage

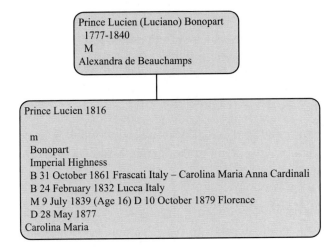

Prince Lucien (Luciano) Bonopart
1777-1840
M
Alexandra de Beauchamps

Prince Lucien 1816

m
Bonopart
Imperial Highness
B 31 October 1861 Frascati Italy – Carolina Maria Anna Cardinali
B 24 February 1832 Lucca Italy
M 9 July 1839 (Age 16) D 10 October 1879 Florence
D 28 May 1877
Carolina Maria

JULIA PIACENTINI

Birth July/September Qtr 1888 Holborn 1b 680.
Death Jan/March Qtr 1909.
Age 21 years.
Julia was eight years old when her father died.

It is now established she was a Ballerina. The photographs and programmes in the book by the V&A prove it. The photograph of her and Lottie – the Paris Opera House Scene 1 in "The Debutante", and the programme of *Coppelia* prove this, which I used for research.

The dances for this were arranged by Katte Lanner who came out of retirement for this in 1906. This is three years before Julia Piacentini died. She would have been 18 in the photograph approximately. The programme for *Coppelia* proves this and that Julia and Lottie were 1908 Ballerinas. Lottie would have been 21 years of age.

Julia is not mentioned in the 1908 performance.

The photographs are in a Book *Adeline Genee* to mark her centenary exhibition in the Victoria and Albert Museum in London. Adeline Genee-Isitt was a great ballerina with perfect timing and technique. She performed publicly at thirteen years of age in the Empire, Leicester Square with a six-week contract of £20 per week which was continually renewed due to her popularity. Adeline Genee became the first Ballerina to turn Ballet into a profession initiating, along with other like-minded Ballerinas, certification for dancing and teaching dancing. The first performance was when ballet was in decline in the west.

Fine Ballet was produced in the 1840s and a lot of it, but never permanently established ballet. It went out of favour and ballet was only performed with Operas as incidential dances.

Whilst in this period the Edwardian Era Ballet was introduced as large, lavish production for the first ballet in the Alhambra and the Empire, Leicester Square.

Ballets were produced in the Empire, Leicester Square by Katte Lanner – Choreographer, Leopold Wenzer – Composer, C Wilhelm – Designer. Ballets were staged to celebrate Jubilees, Coronations, and International Exhibitions. The Corps de Ballet consisted almost entirely of girls.

Coppelia – Czardas, The Hungarian National Dance.

CHARLOTTE PIACENTINI

The Debutante 1906.

Charlotte was also known as Lottie.
Birth 1881 Sep Qtr.

I have now established more facts about Lottie Piacentini. She was married aged 30 years to Albert F P Kidd 15 years after her father died in 1896 when she was only 15 years old. It is recorded in the December Qtr 1911. One child named Dorothy Kidd was born in 1912 and the family called her Doreen.

Charlotte was 15 years of age when her father died in 1896. It is possible that she started performing ballet at this stage as her age is correct even for those times and children performed as young as eleven. She was initially trained by Sadar Vacani who ran a Ballet School and after that by Katte Lanner, one of the world's most famous Choreographers; for each Ballet she performed in as a Ballerina in the Corps de Ballet for each show.

In the photograph it is 1906; therefore she is approximately 25 years of age when performing in "The Debutante" in the Paris Opera House Scene 1 at the Empire Theatre, Leicester Square, London. The copies of the programmes are all the ones in which she is named with her sister Julia Piacentini.

Lottie performed in *Coppelia* at the Empire, Leicester Square, London in 1908 when she was 28 years of age. Lottie is named in the programmes for the ballet, proving again that she was a Ballerina.

Lottie performed in *New York* at the Empire, Leicester Square, London on October 10th 1911 and is named in the programme. In the programme for December 18th 1911 Lottie is named again but these two programmes state Piacentini. By this time Julia was dead as she died in the March Quarter 1909; therefore, it could have only been Lottie performing.

Lottie performed in each ballet with Adeline Genee as the Star.

Lydia Kynash was another ballet Star mentioned alongside Phyllis Bedells throughout the programmes held by the Theatre Museum in London.

In 1910, Anna Pavlova starred in a ballet at the Empire, Leicester Square.

Lottie's marriage was at age 30 in December 1911. The First World War was 1914-1918 and Charlotte would have been 33 years of age with a daughter of two years.

Lottie's photograph is published in a book produced by the Victoria and Albert Museum. She is in two photographs, one signed, and the other proven by the programme.

Charlotte's husband died in December 1939 as the note shows. Lottie M Kidd wrote to her brother Ernest, the writer's grandfather. This is the period of the Second World War and her daughter would have been 27 years of age.

I have researched all the ballets produced from 1901-1911, which are all the ballets for which there are programmes, some photographs and newspaper cuttings. The cutting for *Coppelia* in 1906 gives a very good review and states that *Coppelia* was brilliantly done and needed no sharpening up or improvement.

I feel that Lottie Piacentini would have been at the Empire, Leicester Square for the whole of her career.

My reason for that is that the whole cast are named throughout the years, some in one ballet and some in others, and the main stars are always the same but I cannot prove this through the programmes as they are only named in the ones I have taken the information from.

LOTTIE'S PERFORMANCES

BALLETS

3rd December 1906 – Empire Theatre – Every evening 8.00
Programme entry – The Debutante – Scene Paris 1935

1. The Rehearsal Room of the Opera House – J Hanker and E Banks
2. Behind the Scenes
3. The Garden of Seraglio – R McCleeney

Lottie and Julia are not mentioned by name in the programme. Pictorial information shows the two sisters with their names on their skirts.

May 14 1906 – Coppelia – Programme entry
Czardas and Mazurka
Dancers, Villagers and Musicians – L & J Piacentini listed on programme

May 21 1906 Every evening 8.00 – Coppelia – Programme entry is the same
The following are entries for both sisters dancing every evening:

The Debutante –Julia aged 20 and Lottie aged 23?

16 July 1906 8.00
17 September 1906 8.00
5 November 1906 8.00
15 June 1906 8.00
15 June 1908 8.00 – Only L Piacentini is listed on the programme
7 July 1908 – L Piacentini listed on the programme
20 July 1908 – L Piacentini listed on the programme
21 July 1908 – L Piacentini listed on the programme
3 August 1908 – L Piacentini
17 August 1908 – L Piacentini is entered on the programme for the ballet.
September 7 1908 – L Piacentini

The programmes are the only copies held by the V&A and I have copies for which I signed a declaration on 10th September 1999. It states no other person had made a declaration for the work.

No one was allowed to copy the actual programmes. The declaration was in order that my own family could be informed of their documents and achievements in the theatre and I could copy them.

BALLET PROGRAMME RECORDS

October 10 1911, New York
Scene 1
Bill Posters Dance – States Piacentini
Scene 2
Soubrettes Dance – States Piacentini
The Daily Sketch

Published three photographs of scenes and the Czardas and Mazurka. Dated May 23rd 1906.

There is a short piece written for the opening night stating it was brilliantly performed and it was an excellent ballet and needed little polishing.

Lottie and Julia were definitely Ballet dancers.

Lottie's career is documented from 3rd December 1906 – 18th December 1911 and six weeks takes you to the end of January and if the show continued on her career would be longer.

Lottie Piacentini.

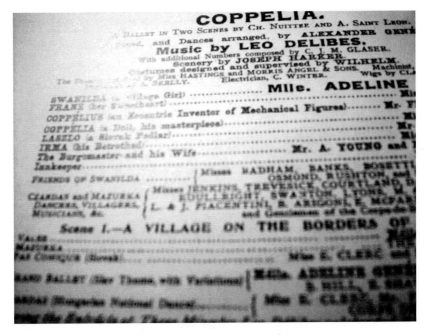

The Debuntante – proving Julia and Lottie's performance.

Coppelia – proving Julia and Lottie's performance.

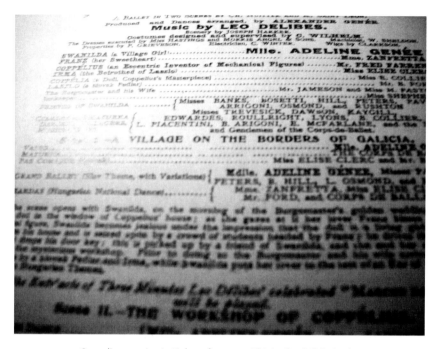

Coppelia – proving Lottie's performance. This is after Julia's death.

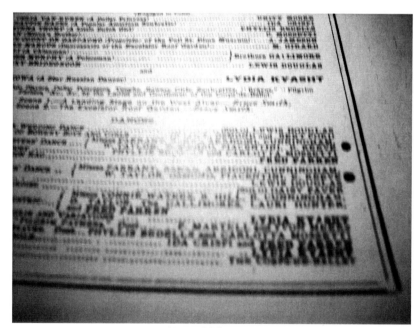

New York bill poster.

Coppelia – Julia and Lottie.

Coppelia – Czardas and Mazavka.

1901 ONLINE CENSUS TRIAL INFORMATION

PIACENTINI

No	Name	Age	Where Born	Administrative County	Civil Parish	Occupation
1	Antonio Piacentini	50	Italy	Monmouth	Newport	Caster Worker
2	Elizabeth Piacentini*	47	Holborn	London	Clerkenwell	
3	Ernest Piacentini	15	Clerkenwell	London	Clerkenwell	Van Guard
4	John Piacentini	23	Clerkenwell	London	Clerkenwell	Coachman
5	John Piacentini*	74	Italy	London	Holborn	None
6	Joseph Piacentini	18	Clerkenwell	London		Glass-blower
7	Julia Piacentini	11	Clerkenwell	London		
8	Lena Piacentini	8	Clerkenwell	London		
9	Martha Piacentini*	69	Cambridgeshire	London	Holborn	
10	Rose Piacentini	10	Clerkenwell	London	Clerkenwell	

* Entries correct and match family history.

All other entries have discrepancies in the age.

All are family except Antonio.

Photo of signatures on marriage certificate – Joseph Albert Victor Piacentini and Jane Adelaide Phillips.

Guiseppe Mencarini.

1901 ONLINE CENSUS TRIAL INFORMATION

MENCARINI

No	Name	Age	Where Born	Administrative County	Civil Parish	Occupation
1	Elizabeth Mencarini*	47	Clerkenwell	London	Clerkenwell	
2	Elleanor Mencarini	13	Clerkenwell	London	Clerkenwell	
3	Henry Mencarini	7	Clerkenwell	London	Clerkenwell	
4	Jennie Mencarini	40	Clerkenwell	London	Clerkenwell	
5	Jessie Mencarini	9	Clerkenwell	London	Clerkenwell	
6	Joseph Mencarini**	49	Holborn	London	Clerkenwell	Printer
7	Lily Mencarini	19	Clerkenwell	London	Clerkenwell	Machinist

* Entries correct and match family history.
** Joseph Mencarini[3]

---

3   Entries are correct and match family history.

CASUALTY DETAILS

Name:	KIDD, Albert Edward
Initials:	A.E
Nationality:	United Kingdom
Rank:	Trooper
Regiment:	Reconnaissance Corps, R.A.C.
Unit Text:	3rd (8th Bn. The Royal Northumberland Fusiliers) Regt.
Age:	20
Date of Death:	22/10/1944
Service No.:	14336249
Additional Information:	Son of Alfred and Martha Kidd, of Stoke Newington, London
Casualty Type:	Commonwealth War Dead
Grave/Memorial Reference:	VIII. C. 11.
Cemetery:	Mierlo War Cemetery

Letter from Lottie Piacentini to Ernest Piacentini posted 11.45 am 15 Jan 1940.

---

24 Stradella Road
Herne Hill
SE 24

I thank you most sincerely for your kind words of sympathy in our recent loss.

The kindness of so many friends has done much to help my daughter and me through this time of great sorrow.

Yours sincerely

Lottie M Kidd
December 1939

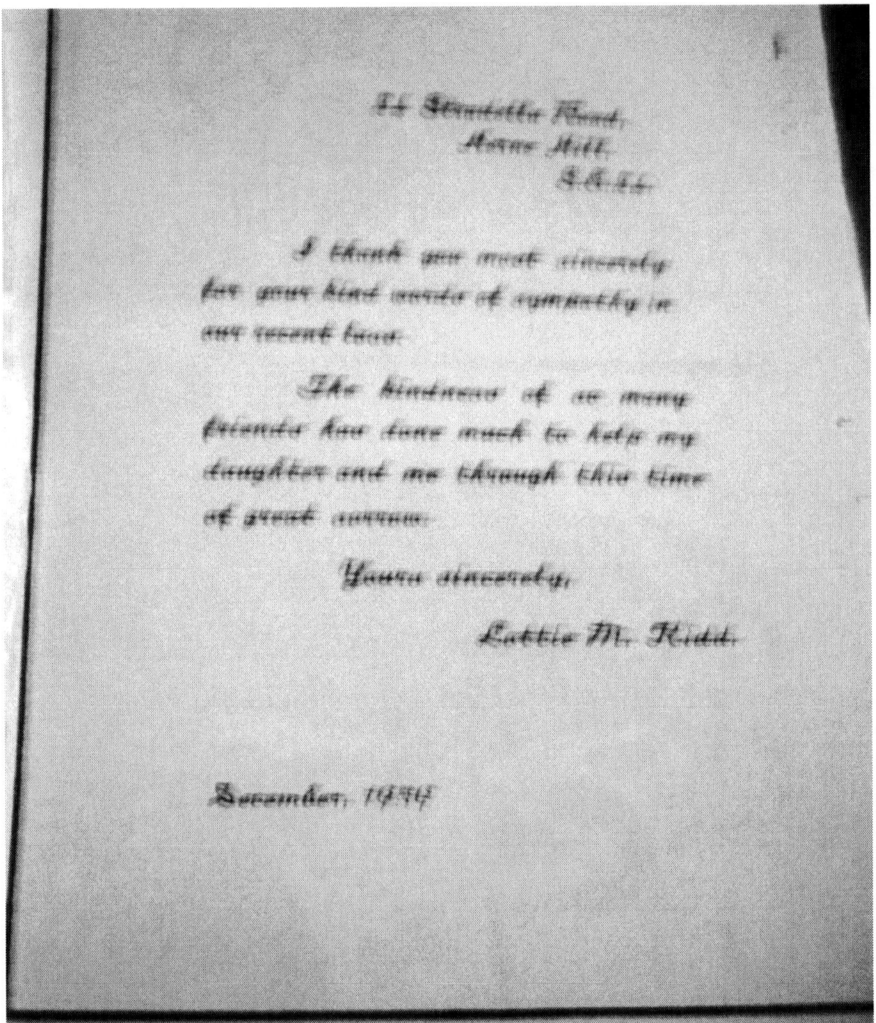

Letter from Lottie Kidd, December 1939.

The ballet "The Debutante" - Lottie and Julia Piacentini.

Catherine Veron Mencarini.

Three Italian Families
Research from Church Records

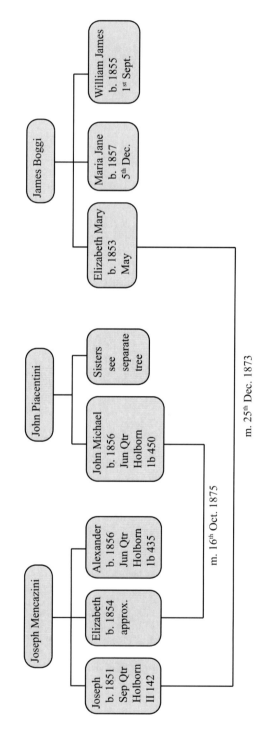

James Boggi

William James
b. 1855
1st Sept.

Maria Jane
b. 1857
5th Dec.

Elizabeth Mary
b. 1853
May

John Piacentini

Sisters
see
separate
tree

John Michael
b. 1856
Jun Qtr
Holborn
1b 450

Joseph Mencazini

Alexander
b. 1856
Jun Qtr
Holborn
1b 435

Elizabeth
b. 1854
approx.

Joseph
b. 1851
Sep Qtr
Holborn
II 142

m. 16th Oct. 1875

m. 25th Dec. 1873

The children of Joseph and Elizabeth Mencazini and the children of John and Martha Piacentini became cousins.

The children of Maria Jane Boggi, whose Marriage Certificate is included for the purpose of interest only, are only cousins to her sister, Elizabeth and her husband Joseph Mencazini.

Births for Mencazini are as follows:

1891. Frederick William Mencazini. Sept. Qtr., Islington. 1b 378.

1891. Jessie Jane Mencazini. Sept. Qtr., Holborn. 1b 691.

Without filing for a certificate, it is impossible to know which child belonged to whom!

NOTE: The whole of this information is as spelt by someone entering records incorrectly and spelling Mencarini incorrectly as Mencazini.

JOHN PIACENTINI

SON OF MICHAEL PIACENTINI

The following are all the known facts about John Piacentini and his family as per the records:

Records consulted:

- St Katherine's House
- London – Births and Marriages
- Alexander House, London – Deaths
- Parish Records
- St Mark's, Clerkenwell
- St Andrew's, Holborn
- Baptismal and Marriages
- London Street Directories

- London Trade Directories
- London Commerce Directories
- London Court Records
- London Census 1851,61,71,81
- Mormon Church Records
- Baptismal
- Records of 1861 Exhibition and 1851 Exhibition in London
- Past Papers Vol. 5 1867-68
- List of Aliens. This lists anyone who has applied for naturalisation since the Act of Parliament was first passed. It also contains Land Registry and many other things.
- City of London Poll Books 1833
- City of London Poll Books 1836
- City of Westminster Poll Books 1836
- Livery of London 1792
- Inhabitants within the Walls 1695

There is no PIACENTINI recorded in any of the records above at any time. Therefore, we can draw the conclusion that the first PIACENTINI in our family to arrive in London was John Piacentini.

I have found a Marriage for another PIACENTINI in the Year 1850, but as yet have been unable to connect that man to our family.

Therefore, I have included a Marriage Certificate for the purpose of interest only.

Records of Melbourn in Cambridgeshire have been consulted but although the FORDHAMS go back until 1583 in the Parish Records there is at no time either for the village of Melbourn or the village of Meldreth any PIACENTINI recorded.

Records consulted:

- Parish Records – Melbourn
- Baptisms
- Marriages
- Banns

- Deaths
- Parish Records – Meldreth
- Baptism
- Marriages
- Banns
- Deaths

Information found:

John Piacentini is recorded in the London Street Directories:

Piacentini John
Glass Silverer
7 Kirby Street
Hatton Garden
Years 1856-1866

IN 1867
Piacentini John
Glass Silverer
Percy Yard 10 ½ Gt Percy Street W.C.
Street: South Side

10 ½ Piacentini John   Glass Silverer –
10 ½ Sabberton Js   Cabinet Maker – PERCY YARD
10 ½ Boulton Joseph   Gas Meter Manufacturer –
10 ½ Fenner Hen.   Shop Front Builder –
These people all shared Percy Yard.

John Piacentini is recorded in London Street Directories

- London Trade Directories
- London Commercial Directories

For these years 1856-1867.

After that he is no longer recorded and nor is any other PIACENTINI.

He does not appear in the Court Records for any of these years or after. He owned a business from 1856-66 in Kirby Street and then moved to Percy Yard in 1867. He had one son and three daughters recorded in the Records Office, St Katherine's House which have now moved to London Records Office – Farringdon. He was the son of a farmer, MICHAEL PIACENTINI.

POOR LAW AND IMMIGRATION ACT – MAP 1889

The map shows areas of London with colour around them to show the wealthy areas and the poor. Hatton Garden, Kirby Street is coloured Red going to a shaded paler reddy shade.

Percy Yard, Percy Street is shown clearly and is a small section on its own next to Clerkenwell Court Sessions. This area too is shaded Red going to a paler reddy shade.

The colours show the wealthiest areas – Yellow which are the royal families' property. The next stage of wealth is Red, then shading to a paler reddy shade. The majority of areas are red plus shading next to it. Poor areas are marked in black like the Rookeries, and the next blue. Therefore, John Piacentini would be classified as wealthy, not poor. Certainly a wealthy tradesman.

1851 MAP OF LONDON shows that Hatton Garden, Kirby Street was not built and Percy Yard, Percy Street was not built at this stage either.

Which confirms my previous research as the Land belonged to a Lord and there was a hospital there. He built the houses in Hatton Garden, Kirby Street for tradesmen.

Glass Silvering was first patented in Britain in 1849 and production did not start until 1850. Glass Silvering was an art known only to the Venetians prior to that time.

The Census Copy shows JOHN PIACENTINI as aged 34. This Census was taken in August 1861. At that time he had three children:-

John 4 years
Elizabeth 3 years
Mary L 1 year

The fourth child was not born until September Quarter 1861 in St Katherine's House according to records – Births St Katherine's House.

There is also a different name recorded in St Katherine's House for the second child Elizabeth!

John Piacentini was born in Chioggia, Italy and Martha Piacentini (Fordham) in Melbourn near Royston, Herts.

John Piacentini signed his Marriage Certificate "In the mark x of" – a sign he could not read and write!

John Piacentini was Married September 10th 1855; his age would have been 28 years. He is stated as 34 years on 1861 August Census.

Banns were called prior to the marriage as it is stated on the certificate and therefore he would have had to be in attendance at church on three consecutive Sundays, meaning that he would have been in England and London approximately 17th August 1855.

His father Michael Piacentini's own birth would be in the region of 1797-1802.

John Piacentini was Venetian by birth. As a tradesman in glass, he could not leave Venice until he reached 25 years of age. At 21 years, he would be a glass-blower and then train as a glass silverer and at 25 years of age could legally leave the Master. Prior to that, he faced a death penalty, to be beheaded, for leaving. Venetian glass secrets stayed in Venice.

MORMON FICHE ENTRY

John Piacentini/Martha
Michael John Piacentini M (marriage) C (christening)
Holborn St Andrews
Event date 8th June 1856

NOTE: Michael John Piacentini is the son of John and Martha Piacentini

CENSUS 1861

Entry

7 Kirby Street
John Piacentini – Head Married Male. Age 34 Glass Silverer. Born Chioggia.
Martha Wife age 29 Born Melbourn, Cambridgeshire
John – son – Age 4 – Born 7 Kirby Street
Elizabeth – daughter Age 3 – 7 Kirby Street
Mary L daughter Age 1 – 7 Kirby Street

The census proves him to be an Italian who married an English woman and that he came from Chioggia, Italy. I have copies of both original documents, having paid for the copies in the records in London. I have not copied for the purposes of copyright.

Marriage of
John Piacentini and Martha Fordham

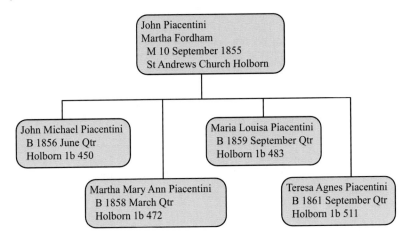

John Piacentini
Martha Fordham
M 10 September 1855
St Andrews Church Holborn

John Michael Piacentini
B 1856 June Qtr
Holborn 1b 450

Martha Mary Ann Piacentini
B 1858 March Qtr
Holborn 1b 472

Maria Louisa Piacentini
B 1859 September Qtr
Holborn 1b 483

Teresa Agnes Piacentini
B 1861 September Qtr
Holborn 1b 511

JOHN PIACENTINI
1881 Census – Saffron Hill District

Information found in the 1881 census.

John Piacentini is recorded with an incorrect spelling of his name – Piacontini.
Other facts about his family are correct.
These facts are given below:-

CENSUS RGU11/0388

Street	Name	Age	Occupation	Where born
33 Forston Street	John Piacentini	54	Glass Silverer	Italy
	Martha	49		Cambridgeshire Melbourn
	Teresa	24	Tie Maker	Middx London

CETTI FAMILY – CENSUS RGU11/0356

Street	Name	Age	Occupation	Where born
73 Myddleton Square	Eduardo (Edward) Cetti		Mathematical Instrument Maker	
	Wife			
	Edward (son)			
	Elizabeth Piacentini	23	Domestic Servant	Holborn

This is Elizabeth, who was recorded in the 1861 Census as aged three; now John Piacentini's daughter is 23 years.

We have at this stage one daughter not accounted for.

NOTE: We have two more Piacentini records on the **CENSUS RGU11/0340.**

Street	Name	Age	Occupation	Where born
15 Red Lion St	ORELLA FAMILY			Lucca Italy
15 Red Lion St	Sabine Piacentini	29 Head Married	Figure Maker	Barga/ Italy
	Amelia Piacentini			Tewklesbury Glos

CENSUS RGU11/0796

Guissepe (Joseph in English) Piacentini – BARGA ITALY
Possibly brother to Sabine but cannot link to our family.

DEATH RECORDS SHOW GIOVANNI PIACENTINI (John) 1904 77 Shoreditch 1c 50 Age 77

NOTE: Tewklesbury on the original document.

FORDHAM FAMILY TREE
TAKEN FROM MELDRETH CHURCH RECORDS

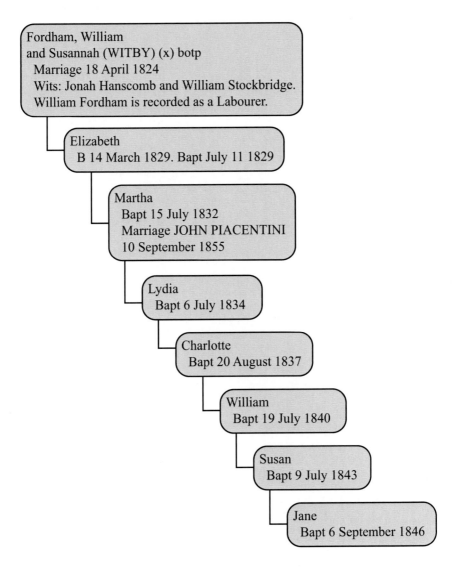

Fordham, William
and Susannah (WITBY) (x) botp
  Marriage 18 April 1824
  Wits: Jonah Hanscomb and William Stockbridge.
  William Fordham is recorded as a Labourer.

Elizabeth
  B 14 March 1829. Bapt July 11 1829

Martha
  Bapt 15 July 1832
  Marriage JOHN PIACENTINI
  10 September 1855

Lydia
  Bapt 6 July 1834

Charlotte
  Bapt 20 August 1837

William
  Bapt 19 July 1840

Susan
  Bapt 9 July 1843

Jane
  Bapt 6 September 1846

Kay Anderson with Carol Oliver (now Ellis) and Rosemary Bush, my bridesmaids, who were not married like myself when the photograph was taken.
The best man, my brother Michael Anderson.

Northern Italy.

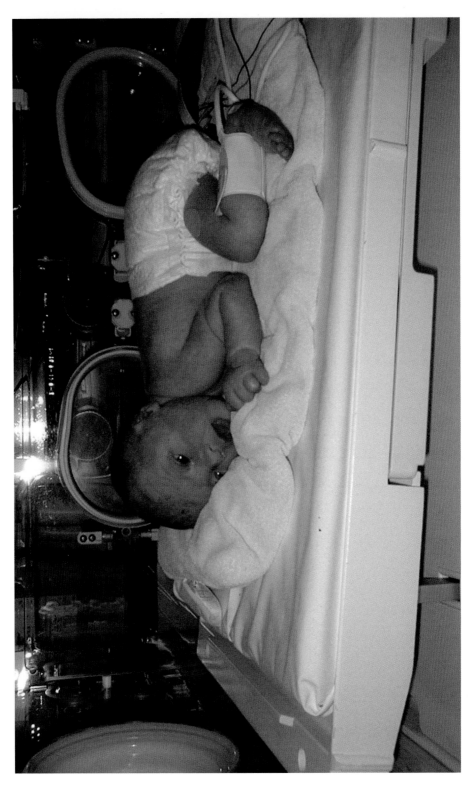

Brandon James Griffiths at Basildon Hospital where he was born.

Brandon James Griffiths.

CHAPTER TWO

PIACENTINI IN ITALY

Venetian Masks.

Mountains and Glaciers.

John Piacentini states in the 1861 August Census that he was born in Chioggia, Italy.

John Piacentini's marriage certificate states Michael Piacentini was a Farmer. John Piacentini was 34 in the August 1861 Census; therefore, his birth year would be 1827.

His marriage was on 10th September, 1855 and he would have been 28 years old. The marriage certificate states the Banns were called prior to the marriage, giving evidence that he was in England on 17th August 1855 as the Banns are called three times on three consecutive Sundays. This would have been the shortest possible period.

As we have documentary evidence of John's trade – Glass Silverer – and his birth place, it is established he was in the Province of Veneto on the Southern end of the Venetian Lagoon!

Michael was between 25-30 giving circa 1797-1802. The fact that John was named John and not Michael, which was a standard practice, implies he was a second son which would still leave us with the same age range for Michael Piacentini if he had children at a younger age.

Having visited Chioggia I was unable to gain a birth certificate.

The area in which farming was carried out in Chioggia, Italy was in the region which is now known as Sottomarina. Going back in time this area was the Orchards, supplying the whole of Italy with fruit.

The town of Chioggia goes back in time and was always a Fishing Port. It is the third largest fishing port in the whole of Italy today.

Both areas are separate islands and are linked by a causeway. If you consult a map of Chioggia you will notice that the Piacentini name appears nowhere on any of the street names which are named after people's families.

The Napolenonic Campaigns Map 1796-7-1800 of the Valley of the Po shows Chioggia and I have an engraved copy which I purchased for historical evidence. When you consult Jacopo Gastaldi's map of South-East Europe 1566 you will note that Chioza and P de Chioza are mapped. There is a difference in the spelling.

When you consult the Census 1861, you will note spelling is Chiogga. I have seen it written Chiozzia and also Chioggia.

EXTRACTS:

- 1797 Napoleonic invasion – Freed Jews from the Ghetto. Jews, "Liberty, Equality and Fraternity."[1]
- May 1797 Napoleon ruled Veneto, and Venice. Autumn 1797 France handed Venice and Veneto over to Austria.
- Venice had 17 years of Austrian rule.
- 1848 – 1 year uprising was put down due to Cholera epidemic.

---

1   It is a motto.

- 1860 – Tuscany, Romagna, Parma and Modena voted to join a United Italy.
- 1866 – JEWS BECAME FULL CITIZENS when Venice became part of Italy.
- Bibliography.
- Insight Guides to Venice 1993 APA.

NOTE:

- 1090 – Venetian Lagoon – Island Guidecca – Unofficial Jewish Community.
- 1516 – Ghetto given to Jewish community ringed with Canals like a moat and prison and the gate closed at night. Trade took place in the day but only by merchants visiting the island.
- 1655 – 5,000 in Ghetto; they were not allowed to buy property; wealth was shown by clothes and jewellery.
- Approximately 1755 – A century later only 1,500 poor in numbers and capital; their tax burdens led to bankruptcy.

The extracts prove that Michael Piacentini was not likely to have been Jewish as he would have lived on the Island de Guidecca – the Jewish Ghetto – and not been allowed to buy land or property. He could only have traded during the day with visitors visiting the island. Napoleon freed the Jews in 1797 from the Ghetto. His occupation was as a Farmer and not a Merchant.

Michael Piacentini was Venetian as he lived in Veneto; according to old maps, he would have lived under French Rule and then Austrian as Napoleon gave Veneto to Austria in autumn 1797 who ruled for a period of 17 years, making this circa 1814.

John Piacentini was born in Chioggia in the province of Veneto; therefore he would be a Venetian. His father Michael Piacentini would have survived Napoleon and Austrian Rule.

After this period of time we can tell no more about Michael Piacentini and cannot establish the fact that he was alive when the states united with Italy or when Jews became full citizens.

NAPOLEON

"Napoleon gave men who served in his campaigns in Italy until the end, plots of land along the 'Valley of the Po'; the land was sandy soil and not well drained; therefore, they had a hard time making a living but some did very well."

Bibliograpy, Insight Guides to Venice.

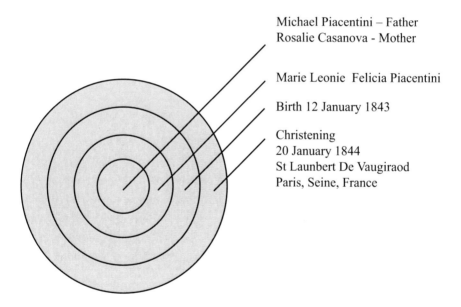

Michael Piacentini – Father
Rosalie Casanova - Mother

Marie Leonie Felicia Piacentini

Birth 12 January 1843

Christening
20 January 1844
St Launbert De Vaugiraod
Paris, Seine, France

NOTE: Michael Piacentini has a son born in Chioggia, Italy and a daughter born in France. She has been christened there. His wife is from the Casanova family.

COAT OF ARMS

GRANTED IN ITALY

Piacentini di Bologna – Arma: Di Nero alla banda seaccato di rossa e d'argento di tre ala coi cape d' angelo.

Translation:

Coats of Arms

Granted in Italy

Piacentini of Bologna – Arm: Of Black to the band seaccato of red and silver of three wings with the angel chief.

Piacentini di Castlefranco – Veneto – Originaria di piacenza, trapi- atata in castlefranco circa il 1370, diede provveditori alla partria, notari, nomini d' arme, cavalieri e scienziati(E-stinta) – Arma di rosso, al leone d'oro.

Translation:

Piacentini di Castlefranco – Veneto – Original of Piacenza, trapiatata in Castlefranco approximately 1370, it gave provveditori to the partria, notari, nominations of arms, knights and scientists (Extinguished) – Arm of red, to the gold lion.

Piacentini di creola e selvazzano nel padovano – originaria da andito di piacenz e trapiantata in –padova nel medioeva, dove fu chiamata, prima piacenza e poi Piacentini, mentre nelia madre patria era conosciuta col nome di Paccagnoti – il primo di questa famiglia di cui si zebra il ricorde e jacopa per due volte podesta di padova nel 1210 – 1247 il quale rice-vette in feudo e vassallaggio dai Coati e dai Maitraversi di padova I beni molini e castelli delle ville di creola e selvazzano, e fu inseritte tra I nobilli cittadini padovan – Bartolomea Piacentini nel 1390 venne da Francesco I da Carrara, constituo pretore della Carta Carrararese per ia sua probita e giuatizia- ara zzurre e di rosso.

Translation:

Piacentini of Creole and selvazzano in the padovano – original from andito of piacenz and transplanted in Padova in the medioeva, where it was called, first Piacenza and then Piacentini, while nelia mother native land was known with the name of Paccagnoti – the first one of this family of which the zebra ricorde and jacopa for two times podesta of Padova in 1210 – 1247 which received in feudo and vassallaggio from the Coati and from the Maitraversi of Padova the assets molini and castles of the Creole villas and selvazzano, and was inseritte between nobilli city padovan – the Bartolomea Piacentini in 1390 it came from Francisco from Carrara, constituo pretore of the Carrararese Paper for ia its probita and giuatizia- it plows zzurre and of red.

Piacentini di Verona – antica fregiata del titolo comitale palation – Nei 1350 vilea un Antionio Piacentini celebre medico, – Francesco e Gabriele ottennere l' aggregazione ei nobile Consiglio, il primo nel 1438, e l'altre nel 1494 – Estinta nel 1543 , ed I suei beni passarona per aredita'nei , Fumanelli – Arma Partito: nel 4 * di rosso, alla stella d'oro: nel 2* d'azzuro , alla fascia d'argento, accompagnata da due stella d'oro una in capo , ed una in punta – alias: Di rosa , alla croce di S. Andrea di di nero, accantonata da quattro stella d'oro.ed I suei beni

Translation:

Piacentini of Verona – ancient fregiata of the title it comita them paption – In the 1350 vilea a Antionio Piacentini celebre doctors, – Francisco and Gabriel to ottennere the aggregation ei noble Council, the first one in 1438, and the others in 1494 – Extinguished in 1543, and e suei aredita assets passarona for in I, Fumanelli – Arm Separated: in the * of red, to the gold star: in the 2* of azzuro, to wrap of silver, accompanied from two star of gold one in head, and one in tip – alias: of rose, to the cross of S Of black, set aside Andrea from quattre star of oro. Ed the sei assets.

HISTORICAL FACTS

List of Jewish surnames in Venezia checked. Piacentini is not listed. Therefore, we are not Jewish at that point in time and not in that area.

1784 Census Leghorn

Princely House of Rospiglios

1700s 1 Piacentini born

1800s 18 Piacentinis born

1900s 19 Piacentinis born

A total of 38 Piacentinis born in 200 years.
Jacapo Francesco Piacentini.
1176-1754 = 78 years.
University of Padua.
Mayor of Padua in 1210-1217.
Notable bearers of the name and noble homes in Bologna, Venice, Verona, Vicenza:
Diaisia Gregario Piacentini – 1684-1754 religious and Professor of Spanish language.
13th Century Barcello Piacentini – Architect.
The name was introduced to the United States as early as 1881 and there are records of an earlier settler.

Immigration of a Miss Piacentini who departed aboard the *Canada* and arrived in "New York" June 22 1881 is a statement made on a document I have.

1880 US Census:
Birth Joseph 1831 Age 49.
Birth Martha 1854 Age 26.
Hamburg Calhoun Illinois.
He is a Farmer and his wife is Keeping House.

THE COAT OF ARMS

The coat of arms that I have is copyrighted 19th February 2002 on my certificate and was granted to the Piacentini family from Bologna. This coat of arms is an artist's impression of what it is like.

ORIGINS OF THE NAME PIACENTINI

This is habitation origin – place of residence of the original bearer of the name, town or village.

Piacentini comes from Northern Italy, Piacenza the town.
The place name is derived from the Italian word "piacente" meaning "pleasant place".

Two names were given. The surname "Piacentini" and a forename to distinguish between each different child born – Piacentini – male/Piacentini – female.

You could have six different boys and girls born; therefore a name is needed for each individual child.

First Crusade, Piacenza – 1802, Napoleon's Army

Having searched using an internet site, the statement made on it says Napoleon sent all young Piacentinis from Piacenza, which was divided into sectors for Piacentini and Piacentino, to fight in Russia, Spain, and Germany.

City of Piacenza

Piacenza was built and divided into sectors, each sector for the different families to live in. Each family name lived in a sector of the city; Piacentini was separate from those using Piacentino.

Italian titles:

- Rarely used before the 13th century
- 14th century titles became hereditary in most of Italy
- 1812 – comital fief (a county) purchaser – became a count

Latin Root, Middle Ages – Baroni

Title of nobility referred to holders of nobilicary rank and holders of feudal property. Seigneuries were in the main elevated to baroni's.

- In 1800 recognition resulting from royal prerogative.
- Not honorific privaligue by wealthy landowner.
- Sons of Baroni could no longer appropriate the title of signore or Cavalerie as a courtesy title.
- Younger son of a Baroni and heir before succession is a nobile dei baroni (seat), a noble of a place.

Piacentini – di Piacentini therefore is the son of the Baroni (Baron), Piacentini being a sector of the city of Piacenza.

Heraldic coronet of a Baron in a jewelled circlet of gold surmounted with seven pearls supported by stems or placed directly upon the rim.

Signore (from the French) introduced 11th century by the Normans.
Feudal Lord Title introduced by the Franks and the Normans.
The younger son of a marquess and heir before succession to the title is a nobile dei marchese di (seat), seat meaning place.

A minor peerage.
A sub-fief attached to a Baron.
Lowest title which carries a seat.
Analysis – Baron – father – sub-divided land.
Two sons example.
Signore – eldest – marquess.
Younger – nobile dei marquess di.
Signore Piacentini – becomes marquess – hereditary title.

PIACENTINI DI CASTLEFRANCO VENETO- STATES ORIGINATES DI PIACENZA 1370 STATES CAVALIER (KNIGHT).

Count – eldest son.
Youngest son – nobile dei conti (seat) noble of the counts of a place.

Counts Palatine were created by certain sovereigns and popes. They were territorial. Just Count and their surname.

Heraldic coronet of a count is a jewelled circlet of gold surmounted by nine visible pearls supported by stems or set directly upon the rim.

CAVALIERE

Hereditary Knight Bachelor – much older than British baronetcy. Mostly descended from younger sons of peers in titled families ennobled with this form of knighthood in the 15th and 16th centuries in Sicily, Sardinia and some parts of mainland Italy. (Researched on internet.)

Piacentini di Castlefranco – Veneto – originating from Piacenzia 1370 circa.

This proves Piacentini had the title prior to that period of time and is a son who has inherited his title, probably the eldest.

The Golden Bull – 1084, Alexius Commeus

Granted Venetians freedom from tributes and imports, a full income, liberty of commerce, exemption from Greek jurisdiction and appropriation for the church of St Mark, an income from the Doge with the title of protosebastas.

Piacentini has arma russo Red with a golden bull which is stated as Di roso al leone de ora. This is a lion.

Francesco Carrera, Lord of Padua, on land 1379 wanted to make peace but conditions were exorbitant. Bartolemeo Piacentini I married Francesco I de Carra 1390; therefore she is the wife of a Lord.

In 1406, Padua and all the possessions of Francesco Carrera were taken and the prince and his sons strangled in prison. He is recorded as a Prince in the Catholic Encyclopaedia – Venice.

France occupied 1509 Cremona.

Duke of Ferrara seized part of Venetian territory 1511. The pope formed the Holy League who were against the Duke of Ferrara.

Nicola Piacentini

Son of Antionio Piacentini born about 1613 (archive date) Barga, Lucca, Italy.

Nicola Piacentini and Caterina Piacentini Married about 1644 Lucca, Italy.

Children – Giovanni Piacentini Birth 25 August 1645.

Assuming Nicola is age 25 in 1645 means his birth is circa 1620. Assuming that his father was 25 years of age, the birth of Antionio in 1595 is approximate.
Taking Nicola as 20 = 1640
Antionio father 20 = 1620
Antionio born about 1613 (archive date)
Could have been born in 1620 or 1640.

Antionio di Piacentini – Verona Medico 1350.

Bologna nobile no date.
Castlefranco 1370.
Creola and Selvazzone Padovana 1390.

Jacop Piacentini 1210 – 1217.

Antionio Male. Birth 26 June 1704 Pacetto Di Valenza Alessandria Italy.
Antionio Birth about 1657 address as above.
Birth 5 March 1862 address as above.

Palace of exposures (FOUND ON AN ITALIAN WEBSITE)
Mentioned as planned from Devout Piacentini and realized in 1883 in order to receive Modern the Museum National d'Arte transferred to goes them Julia in 1914.

Translation – "to goes them Julia in 1914."

From this, I would understand the Palace transferred to Julia, my great aunt Julia Piacentini who was a Ballerina. The Palace became a Museum of National

Art "de Arte" in 1883 and 1914 is when the transfer took place.

(Because of the translation from Italian to English, sentences do not always make sense!)

My great aunt was 21 years of age when she died; therefore no property could have transferred to her. I wonder who took possession as it was the First World War. 1914-1918 I think the Italian government would have seized it. She was in England. She was single and had no children. Other brothers and sisters existed and could have inherited and her grandfather was alive. Was she the only Julia Piacentini? Have they got the Palace today and is Julia Piacentini exhibited in it?

Genealogy always leads you into another direction where you can research and this is an example of it.

Son of Giovanni Piacentini and Gonnella.

Giovanni Francesco Piacentini.

b. October 1st 1679.

m. Marie March 10th December 1705.

Two Children.

Giovanni Pietro Piacentini March 21st 1706/7 Barga,Lucca, Italy (archive date).

Maria Domenico Piacentini 22nd October 1711.

Giovanni and Dominica Piacentini.

Seven children.

Pellegrino b. 17th February 1681/82 archive date.

Nicola b. 17th November 1670.

Caterina b. 19th February 1683/84.

Domenico 6th February 1673/74.

Giovanni 19th January 1671/72.

Nicola 4th December 1676.

Giovanni Francesco 1679.

All children are born in Barga, Lucca, Italy.

Bartolomeo Piacentini.

Sex: Male.

Birth 23rd April 1738

Barga Lucca Italy.

Father Lorenzo Piacentini.

Mother Lucia Giutini.

Caterina Piacentini.
Sex: Female.
Birth 19th February 1684.
Barga, Lucca, Italy.
Father Giovanni Piacentini.
Mother Domenica Gonella.

Taken from a different archive.

1750-51 Anna-Maria Piacentini.
Birth 14th April 1750.
Birth 16th November 1751.
Marriage about 1780 Barga, Lucca, Italy Age 29 years.

Fiorani Giuseppe – His descendants are given below:

Ambrogio.
N 1738 Fermo.
+01.12.180.3
S. Benedetto (Mastro).

Giuseppe.
(Falegname).
N.08.07.1772.
Ripatransone.
+23.03.1853.
S.Benedetto.

Anastasio.
N 17.08.1809 + 25.10.1866.
S.Benedetto.
(Priore Comuunale di S.Benedetto.
Vice Console di Spagna.
Parma – Piacenza).

Piacentini – Rinaldi.
Agostino.
Di Giuseppe e Cerretti Agnese.
N 20.12.1830 Roma.
+ 27.05.1869 Collevecchio.
(Avvocato).

Piacentini – Rinaldi.
Carlo.
Di Giuseppe e Cerretti Agnese.
N 7.08. 1852 Roma.
+ 01.11.1915 Roma.

Piacentini – Rinaldi
Giuseppe.
N 1881 – 16.02.1935 Roma.
Sposa Iandolo Flora di Alessandro.

NOTE: Piacentini-Rinaldi family tree goes back to the **Romans. Alexius Commeus.**

Bartolomea Piacentini married to Francesco I da Carrara.

1317 – 1352   Obizzo III Signore di Ferrara (1317-52) and Modena (1335-52).
1352 – 1361   Aldobrandino III, Signore di Modena, vicar of Ferrara (1352-61), son of Obizzo.
1361 – 138   Niccolo* II, son of Obizzo.
1388   Obizzo IV., son of Aldobrandino, beheaded 1388.
1388 – 1393   Alberto I, Signore di Ferrara, Modena e Reggio, illegitimate son of Obizzo.
1393 – 1441   Niccolo III, illegitimate son of Alberto.

1397 Nicola III married at 14 years of age Gigiola daughter of Francesco II da Carrara, Signore of Padua.

1405 Nicollo* has a son Ugo – illegitimate and his first marriage is childless.

1416 Gigliola da Carrara died of the plague leaving no children.

1429 Nicolo's illegitimate son Leonello was the heir of Ferrara Born 1407.

He took part administratively at the University of Ferrara which had 30 students in the 1430s and 300 students in the 1440s.

* **NOTE:** The spelling differences might well have been a way to distinguish between the generations.

Bovolini (hour Pinarello).
Memory of the ancientness of the said,
the beginning of the sec. XIII, they are l
years of the '200, l'omonima church and
In the Village of Treviso, beyond to the
Community between 1574 and 1580 or
palaces of the Piacentini and the Colur
Paradise, the palace of the Corner is pl:
farm, colombara and rusticali. In the l
l'impianto of the Corner factories and the
endure one d'un twin palace of the previ
and refined all'italiana garden, crowned

Interesting comparto of the Musile (the north-western field) where, beyond to the remembered house of the Barbarella, it is insediata, nearly to ridosso of walls, the house of the Costanzo (committenti of the Shovel of Giorgione), traditionally identified like first city president's house in medieval age.

In pressed dell'incrocio between the two street aces insides to the town-walls building they are places the podestarile palace, or prethorium to you, constructed all'inizio of the sec. XV, and the Mount of Mercy (rebuilt around to the half of the century), beyond which, on the situated dell'attuale piazzetta Dome, erge the said Romanesque church of within.

On the public square of the market, to its western extremity, they show oneself, between the others, the dominicale house, with brolo, of Spinels and cinquecentesco l'edificio, frescoed in facade, dell'Hosteria to the Sword, property of the Piacentini family.

Of the two alignments of factories of the Fortification it orients them, is sure that before one walls to document the census to them of the castellani citizens, in particular of the Pulcheri families (palace hour Bordignon Favero), Novello, Guidozzi (both hour Popular Bank of Castelfranco Veneto) and Bovolini (hour Pinarello).

Memory of the ancientness of the said, for l'appunto, old Fortification, because built up already at the beginning of the sec. XIII, they are l'antico hospital for poor of S. Giacomo, erected in the first years of the '200, l'omonima church and convent of You use (joints to Castelfranco around to 1390).
In the Village of Treviso, beyond to the convent of the Cappuccini, constructed to expenses of the

is supported expenses and in th
lecay is stated passively or qui
:matic situations of such proce:
s appear numerous. Meaningf
:r, from part of the manufactur(
velling (Piacentini property); th
Conservatory) to ridosso of th
le century, one is opened doo
nenico Riccati in the quarter (

The above are sections from my prior book referring to the palaces and property of the Piacentinis in the early centuries.

CHAPTER THREE

TRACING YOUR ITALIAN ANCESTORS

Northern Italy.

INTRODUCTION

Many people will have Italian Ancestors.

They may have Anglicised the name or changed it by Deed Poll. The family who originated in Italy will have emigrated not just to the U.K. Throughout the wars in Italy they may have gone to a wide variety of countries, i.e. France, Germany, U.K., U.S.A., Canada, Brazil and Argentina.

It is not an easy task; you need to enjoy the vast wealth of records available; enjoyment of history will help a lot.

It must be remembered that Italy was all separate countries with their own nobles governing them. In 1866 Italy unified and became one country. The country was without nobles running it any longer. Records previously were in individual countries kept by parish priests in communes.

The first census was taken in 1833 and was the start of national records being kept. Talking to everyone in the family helps a lot. You may find that they do not know enough. My mother never knew exactly where they came from in Italy nor did anyone else.

You may find that contacting Anglo-Italian FHS of which I am a member will help you. There are quarterly books issued and you can purchase them. They have a good website. Some members may have the same interest as you, meaning the same surnames, and already have extensive research.

My younger son was always very interested in the family history and spent time on holiday; I visited Chioggia with him, where my ancestors came from. Adrian went to the archives in Cambridge and searched with me. Whilst at

Canterbury University he checked the records. It was later in time that I discovered the noble background for the name.

You can incorporate it into your holidays and days out. The Family History Fair is very good in London and Fairs are also held in different parts of the country. You will find lots of societies there. The Society of Genealogists has a stand.

I hope you will find my book interesting and helpful and you will enjoy the time you spend researching.

My thanks to the family who purchased a copy of my own family history published for them.

My thanks to Camden Local Studies Library for exhibiting my family history which was donated freely in the "Little Italy" Exhibition 3rd June to 27th September 2008. It has been read by many, but it is not available to copy from or print due to copyright restrictions and not to be taken and printed in any way.

Thank you to all the friends, family, colleagues and club members who took part in lectures on my family history and the discussions on it in my home.

I hope my son Stephen enjoys this book; he is my eldest son.

My grandson, four years of age, is not yet old enough to read it. Perhaps in the future he will be able to read it and enjoy it.

CHURCH RECORDS

They are very different in style from the PRO. They show the date of the child's baptism, sex and the names of both parents. The child's godparents are recorded. The records I studied were Church of England as all Italians are not Catholic. Do not omit to look at Jewish and Catholic Records if unsure of your faith. Local record offices, e.g. Cambridge, have smaller books that are easier to research.

National Archives PRO – Births

Wine coloured books. London PRO was the one I used and each year is in quarters. Listed are surnames, forenames, and sex of the child, month and day. This will give you the parents of the child. Twins are not noted as twins and are not always directly under each other. This only shows one Italian family, possibly two.

Marriages

Green coloured books. Books are in quarters for each year. Marriage certificates which you can order as with birth certificates, will give you more information showing bride, groom, one parent of each; witnesses may be sisters, brothers, cousins, or other parents. It will show more than one Italian family or a mixture of English or Italian.

Deaths

Black books in quarters. Only one Italian recorded. Woman's name is the married one but the maiden name is shown; therefore, you can gain another Italian name, or just one if an Anglo-Italian marriage. If the witness is a daughter it is possible to gain another Italian name and family.

Wills

Very useful and interesting to know of your ancestor's estate. It will give as many names as inherit.

Records of aliens

I chose the Guildhall Library, London which has excellent archives. The records of London aliens were there and I did not find my Italians listed as I found they arrived in the UK in much earlier times.

Other areas have lists of aliens so do not overlook them. Look at the area the Italians lived in on your documents. Check your Central Library – Plymouth, Cambridge, etc – and look at their list of aliens.

NATURALISATION RECORDS

Public Records office at Kew. Many Italians did not naturalise and prior to the First World War there was no legal requirement to do so. As my family were here prior to that they did not have to do so.

If a man joined the British Navy, as did one of my ancestors, they had to naturalise. It is well worth checking. You can order a copy of this document which gives details of his family, background, and dates which correspond with births, marriages, baptisms, and where he came from in Italy in detail. Remember at the earlier dates in time, no women were in the navy.

ITALIAN B.M.D.

Napoleon was the first person to establish a national recording of all births, deaths and marriages. He took a census and recorded all the details on documents which are also archived.

1833 which was just prior to the 1866 Unification of Italy. The Archivo del Stato was started and is excellent. If you do not speak the language, get a small Italian/English Dictionary to help you. Check from other documents you have, the area your ancestor lived in. Use a map to locate the area of the country. Italians lived in communes and the Website holds commune records. Prior to this, it is the local priest who recorded everything. Do not forget that each area which is now a State, e.g Venezia – Republic of Venice – was a separate country with a ruling noble. Weddings were in Church.

After Napoleon took over and ruled with a Monarchy there are records of nobles' coats of arms.

There is an excellent website run by Prinz Karl Fredrich von Deutschland. The Imperial College of Princes and Counts of the Holy Roman Empire.

The Grand Reichs-Chancellor's Office, Royal Mail Post Office Box 276, Teddington, Middx, TW11 1OU, United Kingdom.

This website shows a list of Italian nobles; it contains other countries. **Gianluigi Ravignani De Piacentini (noble of the Holy Roman Empire).**

NOBLES

UK Institute of Heraldic and Genealogical Studies. Northgate, Canterbury, Kent.

*   Books
*   Libro d'Oro della Nobilitas
*   Spetic's Encyclopedia Storico-Nobiliare Italima
*   Scorza's Encyclopedia Araldica Italiane
*   Crollanza's Dizionario Storico-Blasionic della famiglie nobili et notabili Italain

Crollanza's where the entries for my own family name Piacentini are recorded.

It is written in Italian and states the arms, colours and designs. ('Cavalieri' means knight in English.) Dates are given, battles mentioned; Carta Cararese Bartolomea Piacentini married Francesco I da Carrara in 1390. Mention is made of whether castles were taken in battle or lost.

Dates range from 1370, 1210, 1217, 1350 to 1438, 1494, 1543. It mentions Sword, property of Piacentini family. In 1574 and 1580 reference is made to palaces of Piacentini and the Column. Castlefranco was in the hands of Austria until 1805. 1805-1814 part of the Napoleonic Kingdom of Italy. Under Austrian domination in 1814. 1866 Castlefranco with Veneto was united with Italy.

When researching your Italian ancestors remember that they are changing nationality and to look in Austrian records. French archives are helpful too. Napoleon was French.

Archivo di Stalo di Lucca
Piazza Gundiccioni 8
55100 Lucca
Italia/Italy

Other ancient towns have their own archives. Try those in that area.
The Venetian Republic ended in 1797.

BRITISH MILITARY SERVICE

As with many Italian families we have more than one generation in the UK.
Anglo-Italian families' descendants served in the Army, Navy and Air Force.
My uncle served in the 8th Army.

Army records are excellent.

WAR GRAVES COMMISSION

Has an excellent website if dead. You need name, rank, number, division,
unit and regiment. They are very helpful when you write to them.

If alive, newspaper archives. *The London Gazette,* which covers London,
Edinburgh, Glasgow. When checking you will see it is extremely informative
and easy to use, holding WWI and WWII records. You can read the actual
newspapers of the day.

The battle is reported, casualty lists, name, initials, nationality, rank, regiment, unit, age, D.O.B, Service number, parents and address, casualty type
– Commonwealth war dead, grave/memorial reference, cemetery.

You will find promotions; the name is given, old rank and new rank recording reason for the promotion – sergeant, captain etc.

These articles are on all services – Army, Navy, and Air Force.

Medals given are listed. Injuries and names of troops who have been transported home.

The other side of the story is there too. In my case the article I read was how many prisoners of war were taken from North Africa. The article states two Generals were taken and General Piacentini was taken with his troops.

I spoke to my uncle, who was in the 8ᵗʰ Army. A British Soldier whose name was Piacentini, he did not realise either that this General existed, fighting on the opposite to our family's side. Both have the same name on different sides; we do not know if he was related in the past.

Be prepared to uncover details like this: U-Boats sunk, ships sunk, names are given if they know them. Names of hospital ships they are transferred to are given and field hospitals.

CHECK GARIBALDI'S ARMY

Articles in websites on specific towns will give you names of those who joined in that town. My ancestor Michael Piacentini came from Chioggia. Chioggia joined Italy in 1866 on the 15ᵗʰ October. Reading about Chioggia on a website informed me 70 people joined Garibaldi's army of 1,000 soldiers. The youngest soldier was Guiseppe Marchetti who was eleven years old! (Actual count is 1,037 men.)

We would say he was a child unable to join up.

Chioggia was occupied by French troops and passed to Austria in 1798 according to this website. It started to pass over in Autumn 1797. Napoleon ruled in May 1797. Venice had seventeen years of Austrian rule; therefore you need Austrian records in this period of time.

The Laws on Marriage changed. Double wedding means State Ceremony and then Church Wedding by Law.

NOTE: Marriage Double Wedding

If you are English, you relate to this as two couples getting married. Other countries marry whole groups of people at one time. In Italian terms and times there was quite a long period when you had to have a double wedding. You married as a state wedding – non-faith and you married in church afterwards. If you actually married in church first you had a few days allowed afterwards for you to marry in a state ceremony. You had to have special dispensation. When researching in Archivo del Stato you can check both. State and Church records plus special dispensation.

During the Austrian period of rule and then German these countries were not Catholic – therefore they had different views.

WWI and WWII meant no Italian could carry a title. Prior to that we had the French Revolution. Napoleon was French and France ruled in this period of time.

SHIPS' PASSENGER LISTS

My particular ancestor Piacentini came through Le Havre. I had spent a lot of time researching ships' passenger lists.

A lot depends on how much information the Master recorded. Some state only name, age, occupation, and destination. A well recorded record shows name, male, female, age, occupation, steerage, or first class, destination, and sometimes shows whether they have travelled previously to the port. Ellis Island Records are extensive; searching requires selecting ships and dates first; you will have to go through many. Mainly they travel through Liverpool, then back out to USA.

Websites on ships are vast. I used Cyndi's List, which is excellent. It has Italian records of different types on it.

I checked Le Havre records, which are similar and less ships to check but very good records.

England from Boulogne between 1825 and 1858.

Department Des Resources,

Service Interieur et de la Co-ordination,
Service des Archives,
Hotel de ville,
11 Vue de Bertingham,
Boulogne-sur-Mer 62321,
France.
archives@ville-boulogne-sur-mer.fr

Calais – Archives Municipales,
20 Qua De la Gendarmerie,
Calais 62107,
France.
archives@marie-calais.fr

Le-Havre – Archives municipale,
Font de Tournville,
55 Rue du 329 erne,
Le Havre 7662,
France.
archives@ville-lehavre.fr

The ships' lists do not show an Italian or any other nation as a family; you guess by age and name. Italian women are listed, with children and no male. Children of a very young age are travelling alone. Do not overlook children of eleven or thirteen; they are travelling alone emigrating; it does not state who they are going to, only the place.

Le Havre have a register of sailors. A roll, one per voyage, classed according to date of return. It is only French vessels which unload at Le Havre.

Compagnie Generale Maritime was created in 1855. From 1759-1898 there were 600 registers; the original series are on microfilm – 237 microfilms.

In later years, some Italians went to Australia, which is another area of ships' passenger lists you should consult.

DEPORTATIONS

These are listed in the ships' archives but do not overlook deportation in general. Even in 1960 Italians were deported from Denmark. It is a good idea to check Denmark, Sweden and the Netherlands plus Finland. They were deported out of these countries and they were the children of the occupation time. If your ancestor served there it is possible you may find your relative recorded.

Garibaldi's Company in Southern Italy – 1,089 people are named in Giornale Militare of 1864 which was an enquiry by the state committee. These volunteers landed at Marsala on 11th May 1860. It states name, father's name, and home. It is a ship's record. Key in on internet Giornale Militare 1864 and you will get a variety of Websites from which to choose.

NEWSPAPER ARCHIVES

As mentioned previously in detail is the *London Gazette*. The articles and notices are there. Many Italians traded and were in business; they were not ice cream sellers. You will be able to see, sad as it is, bankruptcy notices giving details of the debt, the name of the company and who ran it.

I found my female line Mencarini running a business and trading with China amongst a printed list of people in the *London Gazette*.

Articles on theft and sentences, ships sinking, battles, weddings, funerals – so vast a wealth of information.

I used the *Times* archives, then the *Daily Mail* which goes back later in time. I gained photographic details from the *Sketch* of May 23rd 1906 "Coppelia" and then matched to programmes for my Great Aunts who were ballerinas. One was at the Empire, Leicester Square from 1906-1913. Only one photograph. The General Piacentini article shows a photograph of prisoners with their hands up in the air and British soldiers with them.

Punch archives are there and make interesting reading.

Local newspapers are online and hard copies are kept in local libraries.

3rd June – 27th September 2008
Camden Local Studies Library
Holborn Library
32-38 Theobalds Road
London WC1X 8PA
Little Italy, the story of London's Italian Quarter.

I was invited to the opening ceremony due to the fact I had given a copy of my own book on my family history to the exhibition.

They have newspapers, books and an extensive archive containing photographs of this area and all the Italians living in it.

THEATRE RECORDS

My research took me to the V&A who were extremely helpful. The Victoria and Albert Museum have many programmes and I found my great aunts on the programmes; they wore the most beautiful clothes in very professional ballets. There are other ballerinas mentioned that are Italian. Composers and producers are mentioned, amongst dress designers, even electricians. If your ancestors are in theatre it is a very good source.

They have the archives and the displays on different shows where you can see the costumes, labelled with ballerinas' names, or stars' names. It is an interesting visit but you need to spend time in the archives just reading. Newspaper clippings are there with the show reviews. It stated "*Coppelia*" was brilliantly produced, choreographed and danced. I was thrilled to read such a good review.

I personally did not do La Scala, Milan or the Paris Opera House. They both have records.

Local libraries have books on ballerinas, actors and actresses. Reading a book will often give you information and lead your research in a different direction, along another path of your tree.

CENSUS

Online censuses have made it much easier to research at home without travelling. The advantage is it puts whole families together and shows neighbours as well. Occupations are listed. It was using this type of record that gave me my August 1861 ancestor's family. I was lucky as he stated on it Chiozzia which is Chioggia now, a town in the Venetian Lagoon. My ancestor was Italian we would say now, but was in fact Venetian, and a glass silverer aged 34 in the census.

First you train in a paid for apprenticeship until 21/22 and cannot leave the master until 25 years of age. You were beheaded if you left Venice with their secrets of glassmaking. You could not leave at all until you were over 25 years of age. You would need to prove you were 26. My ancestor arrived in documents – marriage certificate September 1855 age 28. Exact date of arrival must be at the earliest one month prior to Banns being read three times in church, longest time six weeks. This may close your gap in time of arrival in the UK when then researching into ships.

MORMON FICHE

A very good source and all Italians are recorded in UK. You must remember it states parents as well as child but they state event date. The letters are:-

M – Male
F – Female
W – Wife

The next column is:-

C – Christening
M – Marriage

134

Your date is Christening, not the actual Birth date.

I went to the Guildhall Library, London to get a copy which was on microfilm.

Some local libraries do hold Mormon fiches. They have an excellent website, which you can use too. My particular copy goes back in time to 1710. The records they have are worldwide records in the USA. The website gives you access to this vast facility and contact to the Church of the Latter-day Saints.

PHOTOGRAPHS

The first thing to do is look through the old family photographs. Check for comments and names. If you do not know who they are yourself, elderly family members may be able to help you. Match photographs to marriage certificates and birth certificates. Marriage pictures will show a variety of styles of wedding dress.

During WWII, you couldn't get a dress for a white wedding hardly anywhere. Clothing coupons were issued and it was impossible to get enough for a white wedding dress and bridesmaids' dresses. It was not a question of money – it was a government restriction.

Photographs pre-war will show the kind of clothes your family had and this will give you an idea of their standard of living. This should match up with the trades they had. Styles and fashions of the age show too. I have a 1920s' flapper style.

I was lucky enough to come up with photographs of ballets held by other family members and then matched to V&A programmes.

Photographs of soldiers, naval officers and air force members in your family add to your family history and prove your written words.

Fire Brigade

My father served and was in the Blitz. He was not allowed to serve in the forces, as he was an instrument maker with the famous instrument makers Negretti and Zambra.

Negretti and Zambra both came from Italy. They set up business in London and were barometer and instrument makers. My father made instruments for aircraft and rockets and worked with this company for many years until the late 1960s, early 1970s.

Negretti and Zambra have an excellent library of archives on their website with details of the electron microscope my father worked on. You will find they are scientific engineers and many were German.

People worked for them, those who never returned to Germany. Photographs are there as well as text.

Search their website if your ancestor was in this type of work.

Photographs used as postcards are another source. I was lucky enough to find a postcard with a written message on the back and my grandmother's sisters on the front. She was telling her she was coming over to tea. Quite a simple message, giving life to your family history.

Photographs allow you to see how alike you are in looks to your ancestors.

Death Cards

These cards are small with a picture, generally flowers or a cross on the front.

Details on the inside front state the cemetery or crematorium. The next page contains the person's name and death date. It should match your death certificate. I have them for family in Carmen, Manitoba, Canada as well as the UK. I feel it was a standard practice observed. Mine are in the London area. They still make a valuable contribution to your family history. Newspaper articles will match; often there is a short report on the person and what they did for their community. Mine are an Italian family and parts of English as well.

City of London – Poll Books – 1833
City of London – Poll Books – 1836

This is the original Poll Tax paid by people. They are lists of who has paid. It gives the name, address, and amount and they are in Parishes, alphabetically. These are held in the Guildhall Library and are not very big books in size, so are easy to read. From these you will gain Italian names as well as English and others which establish that they lived in the UK and paid their tax.

Livery of London 1792

This is not a big heavy book and lists all the Freemen of the City. As above, it is held in the Guildhall Library. I found my English family names, not Italian. It is still a valuable source of information.

Within the Walls 1695. This book lists all people living in the City of London, which was a walled city, and contains information on families and their trades or as to whether they were servants. Many servants came from other countries. Mainly English surnames. It is still worth checking and the Library in the Guildhall has lots of other books you can use and is a good day's visit.

London Street Directories
London Trade Directories
London Commerce Directories

The directories mentioned are again in the Guildhall Library. If your relative was a registered tradesman/woman he/she will be listed there. Should you not come up with it in trade, it is possible to gain it from the Commerce Directory; the type of business may have been classified more as commerce than trade. You had to pay a fee to enter your details in the book. One may have a lower fee than the other to be entered in.

The Street Directories are for a different reason and you will find Italians listed in them. You need to gain the address from your marriage certificates prior to going to the Guildhall. The Directories are under lock and key. The Librarian will assist you and help if you explain what you want to achieve.

These are old books of the 1800s but they do have later dated books too.

TELEPHONE DIRECTORIES

The very first directories are held in the Library and whilst there it is worth a check. If your ancestor is listed you will feel quite excited as it cost quite a lot of money to have a telephone and be listed. You need your name, address, plus telephone number to cross-reference with your census, marriage certificate and other documents. Thus proving it is your family.

LONDON COURT RECORDS

These are well worth reading and you will see who has been deported and transported, bankruptcy, prison sentences, fines given to people. Prison hulks are mentioned. You will see the ages of people and a description of the crime committed. The crimes range from murder to stealing a loaf of bread. You will be shocked to find they have deported people for stealing a loaf of bread.

Prison hulks on the Thames are mentioned. You will see French prisoners as well as English and Italian.

The crimes mentioned are not as sophisticated as today. The types of fraud, internet crimes and ICT crime did not exist in those times.

Where you have read through you will feel really pleased when research gains nothing for your family name/s. It means you have no criminals in your family tree, even if you think some of the crimes are very minor.

Poor Law and Immigration Law Map – 1889

The map shows areas of London with colour around them. These colours show the wealth or poverty of the area. I was lucky; my area – Hatton Garden, Kirby Street – is coloured Red. Percy Yard is shaded red.

> Yellow – Royal families
> Red – next stage of wealth
> Blue – poorer
> Black – extremely poor (Rookeries)

Just look upon it, if your family are in the blue or black, how far you have come from your ancestors to what you personally are today. This shows your progression and achievement.

These maps are online and you can print out copies.

Coats of Arms

The books listed previously and information given on this subject are available but the information I have is not pictorial. The written word describes the detail. Italy no longer has nobles but coats of arms are passed on to new generations. It is well worth checking with Heraldry at Canterbury who will be able to guide you on copyright and printing of a coat of arms.

Websites

http://www.sevim.it/italianlaaw/index.asp
www.centroruscant – click archivo Diocesi
Then Ricerca nella blanc dati
Enter the surname
Cognome box
Press
Ensugul la ricerca
Scroll down the list until you find the name you want

These are Como Records

http://immigrants.byu.edu/immigrant ancestors' project
archives@ville-lehavre.fr
archives@maireie-calais.fr
archives@ville-boulogne-sur-mer.fr
www.cartedefrances.tm.fr/ insert name in search box – map of France with areas

Distribution of surnames in France
www.rootsweb.com
www.cyndislist.com
http://www.italian-heritage-ancoats.org.uk/ora.html

Andorra Star
www.commune.picisco.fr.it
stpeters-italian-church.org.uk/history.htm
http:/italiangenealogy.tardio.com
www.edit.2000.com/castelfrancov/cennin.html
www.familysearch.org
http://worldconnect.rootsweb.com
Key in search
Ellis Island On-line
Key in search
American Family Immigration History Centre
http://pcturismo.liberta.it
http://www.swordbruden.com

HISTORICAL DATES IN ITALY

1797	Napoleonic invasion - Freed Jews from the Ghetto - "Liberty, Equality and Fraternity".
1797 May	Napoleon ruled Veneto and Venice.
1797 Autumn	France handed Venice and Veneto over to Austria. Venice had 17 years of Austrian rule.
1848	One year uprising was put down due to Cholera Epidemic.
1860	Tuscany, The Romagna, Parma and Modena voted to join a United Italy.
1866	Jews became full citizens when Venice became part of Italy.
1090	Venetian Lagoon – Island Guidecca Unofficial Jewish Community.
1516	Ghetto given to Jewish community ringed with canals like a moat and prison and the gate closed at night. Trade took place in the day but only merchants visiting the island.
1655	5,000 – in Ghetto. Not allowed to buy property; wealth was shown by clothes and jewellery.
1755	1,500 – in Ghetto; not allowed to buy property; wealth was shown by clothes and jewellery.
1914-18	WWI Enlistment and Deportation.
1939-46	WWII Enlistment and Deportation.